Is God Through with Israel?

"Certainly Not!"

Praying Through Romans 9–11

Joan Lipis

Forword by Rev. Malcolm Hedding

Original cover artwork: Mary Jaracz
Top cover photo: Negev Desert by dariazu/Bigstock.com
Bottom cover photo: Grove of orange trees by evdayan/Bigstock.com
Interior formatting: Mary Jaracz

Contact the author at
Web: www.novea.org
Email: Novea@novea.org

NOVEA MINISTRIES

P.O. Box 62592
Colorado Springs, CO 80962

Dedication

To pastors, teachers, and students of the Bible who devote
their days to searching the Scriptures for God's truths,

To those who believe prayer makes a difference and who
use the Scriptures as the foundation of their prayers,

To those who love the God of Israel and His Son, Yeshua the Messiah,

I dedicate this book in the hope it will lead you to a deeper
revelation of God's love for His "firstborn son" (Exodus 4:22).

Contents

Foreword

This work by Joan Lipis concerning the nation of Israel is important because it not only challenges some of the false notions that people hold about this people, like Replacement Theology, but it also sets the biblical position on Israel before us and tells us what, in turn, our rightful biblical response should be.

Joan reminds us, as we read in the pages of this book, that at the heart of everything is prayer: prayer for Israel, the Church, and ourselves. Jesus said that His house should be a house of prayer for all nations, and this tells us something about the strategic value of regular and informed intercession. Prayer is therefore a very powerful tool that is all too often neglected and supplanted in the local Church by other spiritual pursuits. This urgently needs to be rectified, and this work will help us do just this.

This book will draw you back to the essential truths about Israel and the Jewish people, and it will inspire you to live a more inspired devotional life. It is therefore a welcome addition to the many books that have been written on Israel and the Church, and I joyfully commend it to you.

Rev. Malcolm Hedding
Executive Director Emeritus,
The International Christian Embassy Jerusalem

Introduction

Greetings and shalom from Jerusalem!

A hush falls as the sun prepares to set over our golden city. In many homes, families and friends gather around beautifully set tables. With tantalizing smells drifting in from the kitchen, mothers stand to light the candles placed in grandma's silver candlesticks. Fathers bless the bread and wine and pass them around for everyone to have a taste.

It's the Sabbath in Jerusalem!

Although the food recipes vary according to cultural preferences, around the world Jewish people observe the same traditions and recite the same prayers. How did these traditions start? I don't know. Nor do I know where or when they began.

Although I was raised in a secular Jewish home, my grandmother was a God-fearing woman. By God's grace, I inherited that fear of God. Although I didn't know the Bible or even the modern history of Israel, I was content knowing in my heart that God existed and that He knew me.

My initial response to the Gospel was one of extreme antagonism. I felt threatened, as if my identity as a Jew was being challenged. I didn't know anything about Jesus except that He'd been responsible for the persecution and death of Jews for centuries.

All that changed in 1986 when, at the age of 40, I became a follower of Yeshua (the Hebrew name for Jesus). My salvation was the result of seeing an enactment of the crucifixion while Isaiah 53 was read in the background. Recognizing the "Jewishness" of the Gospel made the decision easy. I was instantly filled with the greatest peace and joy I'd ever experienced.

But my "church experience" was anything but joyous.

Being Jewish in the Church

As a lover and follower of Yeshua, I had not lost or changed my ethnicity as a Jew. In fact, I felt more Jewish than before. Believing in Yeshua seemed to complete my Jewish identity. Truly, my salvation was part of the prophetic fulfillment of God's promise that one day "all Israel will be saved" (Romans 11:26).

I was nevertheless confronted, confused, and then challenged by the Church's lack of understanding of the significance of Israel and the Jewish people. Although I saw Yeshua on every page of the Old Testament, many Gentile Christians ignored Israel. Somehow they drew a distinction between the "Israelites" of the Exodus and the Jews of today! One pastor told me that the reason he doesn't teach about Israel is because it's "divisive and too political." A ministry leader and elder in a Bible-teaching church said to me: "Why should I bless a people whom God has cursed?"

And yet, God connects the revelation of His character to His relationship with Israel (Isaiah 43:10). Ignoring or denying this relationship will hinder and limit our knowledge of who God is and blind us to seeing what Paul calls "life from the dead" (Romans 11:15).

Paul's letter to the church at Rome is often considered his ultimate treatise on faith. Yet after an exuberant outburst of praise (Romans 8:37-39), he reflects on God's unique relationship with the Jewish people (Romans 9-11).[1]

When the Apostle Paul poses the question of whether God has cast away the Jewish people because of their rejection of Christ, he answers by using the emphatic Greek phrase οὖν μὴ [*oun mā'*], meaning "Certainly Not!"

But sadly, over the years, I have met many well educated, committed Christians and even ministry leaders who don't share God's perspective or Paul's passion. This attitude has resulted in many Christians becoming ignorant of God's plans and purposes for Israel, resulting in His commands going unheeded and unfulfilled. Some of these commands to the Church regarding Israel include:

- Pray for the peace of Jerusalem (Psalms 122:6).
- Exalt Jerusalem higher than one's chief joy (Psalms 137:6).
- Rejoice with her (Deuteronomy 32:43; Isaiah 66:10-11).
- Care for her people and help rebuild and restore the land (Isaiah 49:22-23; 66:12).

So as my walk with Christ progressed, I was faced with a choice: either ignore my heritage, or leave the Church. Praise God, I did neither. Instead, I chose to dig deeper into Scripture; a seminary education followed. I wanted to understand and then share:

- God's plan for Israel: past, present, and future,
- The distinction between Israel and the Church,
- God's plan for the nations, especially as it relates to Israel,
- The Church's response and responsibility toward Israel.

I believe that as more Christians understand God's plan for Israel and share His heart, they will begin to pray for her salvation. That seems to have been Paul's argument in his letter to the Romans. It is my purpose for writing **Certainly Not!**

Some Definitions:

Some definitions may be helpful at this point.

- I use "Israel" interchangeably to refer to a people, a nation, or a land and use the feminine pronoun "her" to refer to this collective unit.
- A "Jew" (or "Jewish") refers to a person who is a natural descendant of Abraham, Isaac, and Jacob regardless of his or her spiritual condition.[2] A Jewish person can be a religious adherent of Judaism, an atheist, an agnostic, or a follower of Christ.
- "Israelite" is the term used in the Old Testament, but it is rendered "Jew" in the New Testament.
- "Gentile" describes every non-Jewish person regardless of his or her spiritual condition. The Hebrew word for "Gentiles" is translated in the Old Testament as "nations."
- A "Christian" is a person who has accepted Jesus as Lord and Savior and follows Him through trust and obedience. A Christian can be either Jewish or Gentile.
- "The Church," also called "the Body of Christ," consists of individuals who have been saved by God's grace through faith in Jesus, regardless of specific church affiliation, gender, age, nationality, or ethnic background. The Church is the manifestation of the "One New Man" (Ephesians 2:15) that is comprised of Jews and Gentiles united in Christ.
- "Yeshua" or "Jesus." You will find that I use these names interchangeably. Yeshua is the Hebrew word for "salvation," hence Savior. Jesus is the Greek form of Yeshua, arrived at by transcribing the Hebrew and adding an "s" to the nominative to facilitate declension.

"God" or "LORD" is the God of Israel, the God of the Bible, who gives His memorial name to Moses in Exodus 3:14 as אהיה אשר אהיה, translated in the New King James Version as "I AM WHO I AM."[3]

How To Use This Book:

Certainly Not! is a daily prayer guide with commentary that primarily follows Paul's teaching found in Romans 9-11. Sometimes we consider a complete verse. Other times, we take several days to focus on just one phrase. Because of their importance to Paul's arguments, we sometimes examine other Scriptures he references.

For those who are interested in the original languages of Greek and Hebrew, I have included some of the more important theological terms Paul uses. For more precise transliterations, I've found "Blue Letter Bible" to be invaluable (https://www.blueletterbible.org).

Each day builds on the previous day, but can also be read individually. Each daily segment consists of a short commentary, a verse, and a prayer suggestion.

The prayer suggestions at the end of each day are just that—suggestions. I believe that as you pray God's word, the Holy Spirit will guide your prayers (Romans 8:26).

Moreover, I believe that the Word of God is powerful and will accomplish its purpose (Hebrews 4:12; Isaiah 55:10-11). These daily prayers are therefore brief; one minute CAN make a difference.

Keep Praying!

Now that you've begun to pray for Israel, please join our international prayer network. Every day, we send a Scripture and prayer suggestion to email inboxes around the world. It doesn't matter when or where you pray; the power comes from our community praying the same promise in many languages. Subscribe at: www.lunchtimeprayer.com

Thank you! May you experience all of God's promised blessings in Yeshua's name.

With love,

Joanie

Day 1

Paul's letter to the Romans has been considered the ultimate treatise on faith. Chapters 1-8 have been especially significant in the history of the Church.

Yet many Bible-believing churches do not teach from Romans 9-11. The reasons are varied, but I suggest that none are entirely valid. ("The Controversy of Zion" [Isaiah 34:8 KJV] detailing attitudes toward Israel is examined in "The Controversy of Zion", Page 103.)

Chapters 9-11 of Romans have tremendous significance and present the most concise and complete revelation of God's unique relationship with Israel. Nowhere else does Paul give such a detailed explanation of that relationship, share his passion for the Jews, and challenge and caution Gentile believers on their responsibility and response to Israel.

The best way to begin our 90-day prayer journey is by reminding ourselves of God's plan, promise, and purpose regarding Israel. This means starting at the beginning, with the Torah.[4]

Genesis 12:1-3,7

Now the LORD had said to Abram:

> *"Get out of your country,*
> *From your family*
> *And from your father's house,*
> *To a land that I will show you.*
> *I will make you a great nation;*
> *I will bless you*
> *And make your name great;*
> *And you shall be a blessing.*

I will bless those who bless you,
And I will curse him who curses you;
And in you all the families of the earth shall be blessed."

Then the LORD appeared to Abram and said, "To your descendants I will give this land." And there he built an altar to the LORD, who had appeared to him.

We've heard the Jews being called "the Chosen People," but few people know for what and why they were chosen. The answer comes through the prophet Isaiah.

Isaiah 43:10-12

"You are My witnesses," says the LORD,
"And My servant whom I have chosen,
That you may know and believe Me,
And understand that I am He.
Before Me there was no God formed,
Nor shall there be after Me.
I, even I, am the LORD,
And besides Me there is no savior.
"I have declared and saved,
I have proclaimed,
And there was no foreign god among you;
Therefore you are My witnesses,"
Says the LORD, "that I am God."

PRAY FOR THE CHURCH TO ACKNOWLEDGE
AND REJOICE IN GOD'S CHOICE OF ISRAEL.

Day 2

God's unique relationship with Israel is also mentioned in the Writings.[5]

Psalms 89:1-4

I will sing of the mercies of the LORD forever;
With my mouth will I make known Your faithfulness to all generations.
For I have said, "Mercy shall be built up forever;
Your faithfulness You shall establish in the very heavens."

"I have made a covenant with My chosen,
I have sworn to My servant David:
'Your seed I will establish forever,
And build up your throne to all generations.'"

Psalms 89: 30-37

"If his sons forsake My law
And do not walk in My judgments,
If they break My statutes
And do not keep My commandments,
Then I will punish their transgression with the rod,
And their iniquity with stripes.
Nevertheless My lovingkindness I will not utterly take from him,
Nor allow My faithfulness to fail.
My covenant I will not break,
Nor alter the word that has gone out of My lips.
Once I have sworn by My holiness;
I will not lie to David:
His seed shall endure forever,

And his throne as the sun before Me;
It shall be established forever like the moon,
Even like the faithful witness in the sky."

PRAY FOR ISRAEL TO EMBRACE HER UNIQUE
RELATIONSHIP WITH HER GOD.

Day 3

Before we begin our study of Romans 9-11, we must consider the context. Keep in mind that when Paul wrote this letter, there were neither chapters nor verses.

In Chapter 8, Paul is overwhelmed by the goodness of God through Yeshua.

Romans 8:31-35

What then shall we say to these things? If God is for us, who can be against us? He who did not spare His own Son, but delivered Him up for us all, how shall He not with Him also freely give us all things? Who shall bring a charge against God's elect? It is God who justifies.

Who is he who condemns? It is Christ who died, and furthermore is also risen, who is even at the right hand of God, who also makes intercession for us. Who shall separate us from the love of Christ? Shall tribulation, or distress, or persecution, or famine, or nakedness, or peril, or sword?

As Paul is filled with praise for God's faithfulness, he naturally thinks of God's faithfulness to Israel.

PRAISE GOD FOR HIS FAITHFULNESS TO
ISRAEL AND TO THE CHURCH.

Day 4

God's unique relationship with Israel is a reflection of God's character. If God could break His covenant relationship with Israel, Christians would have no basis or reason to believe or trust Him.

Romans 8:38-39

For I am persuaded that neither death nor life, nor angels nor principalities nor powers, nor things present nor things to come, nor height nor depth, nor any other created thing, shall be able to separate us from the love of God which is in Christ Jesus our Lord.

PRAY THAT ISRAEL WILL RECOGNIZE GOD'S
FAITHFULNESS AND TURN TO HIM THROUGH
FAITH IN YESHUA THE MESSIAH.

Day 5

We've taken the time to set the stage and are now ready to dig into Romans 9-11.

Many Jewish people today concede that Yeshua lived as a Jewish man, but believe it was Paul who actually started a new religion. Nothing could be further from the truth. Paul never considered himself to be anything other than a Jew. He lived his entire life as a Jew. And using a Jewish book, the Tanakh (Old Testament), he taught that Yeshua was the promised Messiah and the fulfillment of the promised New Covenant (Jeremiah 31:31).

From the moment of his salvation, Paul spent his life bringing the message of the Gospel of God's grace through Yeshua, first to the Jews and then to the Gentiles. His driving passion was the glory of God and the salvation of his people.

Every person who loves, worships, and follows Yeshua should share this passion.

Romans 9:1-4a

I tell the truth in Christ, I am not lying, my conscience also bearing me witness in the Holy Spirit, that I have great sorrow and continual grief in my heart. For I could wish that I myself were accursed from Christ for my brethren, my countrymen according to the flesh, who are Israelites.

PRAY FOR YOUR CHURCH TO HAVE A PASSION TO PROCLAIM YESHUA AS THE MESSIAH TO ISRAEL.

Day 6

It is a challenge for some Christians to believe the enduring validity of God's promises to Israel when she remains in spiritual rebellion, refusing to accept Yeshua. But God is faithful, His promises are literal, and His unique relationship with Israel has never changed.

Paul reminds us how that relationship has been manifested in the past so we can trust the rest of God's promises for Israel's future.

Romans 9:4-5

[The] Israelites to whom pertain the adoption, the glory, the covenants, the giving of the law, the service of God, and the promises; of whom are the fathers and from whom, according to the flesh, Messiah came, who is over all, the eternally blessed God. Amen.

It's vital to the health of the church that all followers of Yeshua understand and appreciate this unique relationship between God and Israel. Notice that this relationship is based on God's choice of Abraham, Isaac, and Jacob—not on the "specialness" or the faithfulness of the Jewish people.

PRAY FOR THE HEALING OF ISRAEL'S
SPIRITUAL CONDITION.

Day 7

Israel's current rebellion and the following verse have caused two great misunderstandings.

Romans 9:6

But it is not that the word of God has taken no effect. For they are not all Israel who are of Israel.

First, some followers of Yeshua reading this verse have suggested that because Israel remains in rebellion against God, His plans and purposes for her have been thwarted. But Paul already refuted that idea in Romans 8:28-38.

Paul's words in this verse also give rise to a second misunderstanding. Some Gentile followers of Yeshua suggest that they (the Gentiles) have now become the "true" Israel. This misunderstanding is the foundation of what is called "Replacement Theology," which says that the Christian Church has replaced Israel.

In his letters, however, Paul repeatedly defines Israel as the Jewish people, also referring to them as "the circumcised, " to distinguish them from Gentiles (1 Corinthians 7:19; Galatians 2:7). So in this verse, he is merely saying that not all Jews will obey God. Only a remnant—those Jews who love, trust, and follow Him through faith in Yeshua, the Messiah of Israel—will enjoy the fullness of His promised blessings. They are the true sons of Abraham.

PRAY AGAINST THE DECEPTION OF
REPLACEMENT THEOLOGY.

Day 8

Mankind has always rebelled against God's sovereignty, trying to become equal to or like God. This thinking, called "humanism," puts man in the center of the universe and judges God by man's standards. We hear it today in the challenge "God is not fair."

But when we truly understand God's character, the questions and challenges vanish. He is loving, holy, and just. He is the Creator and Sustainer of the universe. Knowing who He is should end all debate over His choice of Israel for a special destiny.

God is the center of His universe and does whatever He pleases.

Psalms 135:6

Whatever the LORD pleases He does,
In heaven and in earth,
In the seas and in all deep places.

It pleased God that His plan of redemption would come through Isaac, the promised son of Abraham and Sarah.

Genesis 21:12

But God said to Abraham, "Do not let it be displeasing in your sight because of the lad or because of your bondwoman. Whatever Sarah has said to you, listen to her voice; for in Isaac your seed shall be called."

PRAY ISRAEL WILL RETURN TO GOD WITH
ALL HER HEART, SOUL, AND MIND.

Day 9

In a time of doubt, Abraham fathered a son through Hagar. Hagar's son (Ishmael) was the fruit of sin, whom Paul calls the "son of the flesh." But Sarah's son (Isaac) was a miracle child, whom Paul calls the "son of promise," referring to God's original promise to make Abraham a great nation that would bless all the families of the earth (Genesis 12:2-3; 21:12).

God also promised to make Ishmael into a nation (Genesis 21:13), but His plan of redemption would come by "promise," not by "flesh."

Paul refers back to Ishmael and Isaac as he explains why "not all Israel is Israel."

Romans 9:7-9

...nor are they all children because they are the seed of Abraham; but, "In Isaac your seed shall be called." That is, those who are the children of the flesh, these are not the children of God; but the children of the promise are counted as the seed. For this is the word of promise: "At this time I will come and Sarah shall have a son."

PRAY FOR THE DESCENDANTS OF ISAAC
AND ISHMAEL TO RECONCILE AND COME
TOGETHER BY FAITH IN YESHUA.

Day 10

Paul's letter to the Romans is one of the most convincing arguments for what is called the "predetermination of God" or the doctrine of "election." This doctrine essentially states that God has determined our lives before we were born, thus eliminating our free will to make our own life choices.

These opposing ideas of free will and predetermination continue to be argued among Christians. Those who believe in predetermination point to these choices made by God:

- Abraham
- Isaac instead of Ishmael
- Jacob instead of Esau
- Israel instead of other nations
- David instead of his brothers

Romans 9:10-12

And not only this, but when Rebecca also had conceived by one man, even by our father Isaac (for the children not yet being born, nor having done any good or evil, that the purpose of God according to election might stand, not of works but of Him who calls), it was said to her, "The older shall serve the younger."

Paul does not doubt God's election of Isaac and his seed as the vehicle through which the Messiah would come.

PRAY FOR ALL THOSE WHO LOVE THE BIBLE
AND THE GOD OF THE BIBLE TO ACCEPT
GOD'S SOVEREIGN PLAN FOR ISRAEL.

Day 11

It may seem easy for us to understand God's choice of Isaac (son of promise) versus Ishmael (son of flesh), but what about Jacob over Esau? They were twins!

Romans 9:13

As it is written, "Jacob I have loved, but Esau I have hated."

The challenge we face here is not only accepting God's sovereign choice, but also His love for one twin and His hatred of the other. How can the God of love also hate? The best way to understand this statement about God's hatred is to look at Esau's (and later Edom's) behavior toward Isaac (and later Israel). We need to remember that from the beginning, God already knows the end.

PRAY FOR THE DESCENDANTS OF ESAU TO RECEIVE GOD'S LOVE THROUGH FAITH IN MESSIAH YESHUA.

Day 12

Paul's final response to the challenges about God's sovereign choices, especially His choice of Israel, is unequivocal and unambiguous. He responds by using a very strong Greek phrase οὖν μὴ [*oun mā'*], which means: ***"NO! Certainly not!"***

Romans 9:14-18

What shall we say then? Is there unrighteousness with God? ***Certainly not!*** *For He says to Moses, "I will have mercy on whomever I will have mercy, and I will have compassion on whomever I will have compassion." So then it is not of him who wills, nor of him who runs, but of God who shows mercy. For the Scripture says to the Pharaoh, "For this very purpose I have raised you up, that I may show My power in you, and that My name may be declared in all the earth." Therefore He has mercy on whom He wills, and whom He wills He hardens.*

God's motivation for everything He does, including each of His choices, is to reveal His character so the earth will be filled with the knowledge of His glory.[6]

Even in her times of rebellion against God, Israel is still His chosen witness. Paradoxically, because of her rebellion, Israel is serving as a witness of God's faithfulness to Himself, His character, and His word.

PRAY THE EYES OF ISRAEL WILL BE OPEN TO SEE
GOD'S FAITHFULNESS AND HER UNFAITHFULNESS.

Day 13

Despite the attempts of mankind (Jews and Gentiles) to be completely separate from God or to find Him "their own way," He is sovereign. Yes, He gives men free will, but ultimately, He is the boss and demands His way.

Jeremiah 18:1-6

The word which came to Jeremiah from the LORD, saying: "Arise and go down to the potter's house, and there I will cause you to hear My words." Then I went down to the potter's house, and there he was, making something at the wheel. And the vessel that he made of clay was marred in the hand of the potter; so he made it again into another vessel, as it seemed good to the potter to make.

Then the word of the LORD came to me, saying: "O house of Israel, can I not do with you as this potter?" says the LORD. "Look, as the clay is in the potter's hand, so are you in My hand, O house of Israel!"

His choice of Israel does not conflict either with Israel's freedom to make choices or with His sovereignty over her.

PRAY FOR ISRAEL TO TURN BACK TO HER
GOD IN HUMILITY, TRUST, AND FAITH.

Day 14

The people in Jeremiah's day challenged the potential ramifications of God's predetermination. People today still bring up the same issue.

This challenge centers on the individual's responsibility in light of God's election, choice, or predetermination. It asks how can God hold anyone responsible if:

- God already knows what that person will do?
- God has already determined what that person will do?

If God is sovereign, then what "right" does He have to criticize or accuse anyone or any nation?

Paul doesn't shy away from this challenge, but addresses it directly.

Romans 9:19

You will say to me then, "Why does He still find fault? For who has resisted His will?"

We'll see Paul's response tomorrow.

PRAY FOR ISRAEL TO SURRENDER TO GOD'S WILL.

Day 15

God addressed the issue of His sovereignty back in Jeremiah's day. Paul refers to the word of the Lord that came to Jeremiah at the potter's house (Jeremiah 18:1-11).

Romans 9:21

But indeed, O man, who are you to reply against God? Will the thing formed say to him who formed it, "Why have you made me like this?" Does not the potter have power over the clay, from the same lump to make one vessel for honor and another for dishonor?

Paul's question is not rhetorical. The truth is that God is patient and will fulfill His plans and purposes in His perfect time. The day will come for the revelation of His glory and blessings to all mankind, both to Israel (the Jews) and the nations (the Gentiles).

Romans 9:22-24

What if God, wanting to show His wrath and to make His power known, endured with much longsuffering the vessels of wrath prepared for destruction, and that He might make known the riches of His glory on the vessels of mercy, which He had prepared beforehand for glory, even us whom He called, not of the Jews only, but also of the Gentiles?

PRAY FOR THE SALVATION OF
ISRAEL AND THE NATIONS.

Day 16

Paul further answers his own question about God's right to make sovereign choices by explaining the mystery of His salvation for the Gentiles. His answer, that God's plan has always included the Gentiles, reveals his profound understanding of the Hebrew Bible.

Romans 9:25

As He says also in Hosea:

> *"I will call them My people, who were not My people,*
> *And her beloved, who was not beloved."*

The full passage in Hosea that Paul is referencing reads:

Hosea 2:23

> *"Then I will sow her for Myself in the earth,*
> *And I will have mercy on her who had not obtained mercy;*
> *Then I will say to those who were not My people,*
> *'You are My people!'*
> *And they shall say, 'You are my God!'"*

From Genesis to Revelation, the Bible is one book!

PRAY ISRAEL WILL SUBMIT TO GOD'S
PLANS AND PURPOSES.

Day 17

When anyone is jealous or resentful of Israel's unique relationship with God, it reveals his or her ignorance of God's love for all people and nations.

Having addressed God's mercy to the Gentiles, Paul turns to God's mercy to the Jews. He continues quoting from Hosea.

Romans 9:26

"And it shall come to pass in the place where it was said to them,

'You are not My people,'
There they shall be called sons of the living God."

Although the majority of Jewish people do not believe in Yeshua, God promised that He would have always have a remnant.[7] Today we are seeing that remnant, as more and more Jews are coming to faith in Yeshua.

Hosea 1:10

"Yet the number of the children of Israel
Shall be as the sand of the sea,
Which cannot be measured or numbered.
And it shall come to pass
In the place where it was said to them,
'You are not My people,'
There it shall be said to them,
'You are sons of the living God.'"

PRAY FOR THE JEWISH PEOPLE EVERYWHERE
TO BECOME THE "SONS OF GOD"
THROUGH FAITH IN YESHUA.

Day 18

Paul reminds the people of Isaiah's warning; a time will come when God's patience ends for both the Jews and the Gentiles. It will be a time when His justice rules throughout the world. He will bring destruction on the wicked, but give grace to those who believe in Him.

Romans 9:27-28

Isaiah also cries out concerning Israel:

> *"Though the number of the children of Israel be as the sand of the sea,*
> *The remnant will be saved.*
> *For He will finish the work and cut it short in righteousness,*
> *Because the LORD will make a short work upon the earth."*

The Jewish people will not be exempt from God's wrath in that great and terrible day.

Isaiah 10:22-23

> *For though your people, O Israel, be as the sand of the sea,*
> *A remnant of them will return;*
> *The destruction decreed shall overflow with righteousness.*
> *For the LORD God of hosts*
> *Will make a determined end*
> *In the midst of all the land.*

PRAY FOR ISRAEL TO LOOK TO YESHUA
AND BE SAVED FROM GOD'S WRATH.

Day 19

Paul warns that God's wrath upon unbelieving Israel will be worse than anything she's ever experienced.

Romans 9:29

And as Isaiah said before:

> *"Unless the LORD of Sabaoth had left us a seed,*
> *We would have become like Sodom,*
> *And we would have been made like Gomorrah."*

His warning echoes the words of the prophet Isaiah.

Isaiah 1:9

Unless the LORD of hosts
Had left to us a very small remnant,
We would have become like Sodom,
We would have been made like Gomorrah.

So that God's warning does not go unnoticed or unheard, it is crucial that we pray and share the offer of God's mercy through faith in Yeshua the Messiah.

PRAY FOR BOLDNESS, WISDOM, AND SENSITIVITY TO
SHARE THE GOSPEL WITH THE JEWISH PEOPLE.

Day 20

Thus far Paul has made two points:

- God offers redemption and salvation to both Jews and Gentiles,
- There will only be a remnant of Israel who will accept His offer of salvation.

Next, Paul begins to address the crucial issue of righteousness: How do we become acceptable in God's sight?

Romans 9:30

What shall we say then? That Gentiles, who did not pursue righteousness, have attained to righteousness, even the righteousness of faith.

The common definition of righteous is *to be morally good, virtuous, a good citizen.*[8] In a spiritual sense, it means *to be approved by God.*

PRAY FOR RELIGIOUS JEWS TO RECOGNIZE
THAT GOD WILL NOT ACCEPT THEIR
ATTEMPTS TO BE RIGHTEOUS.

Day 21

The issue of righteousness is foundational to the Gospel and therefore to Paul's teaching. Hence we repeat this verse for emphasis.

Romans 9:30

What shall we say then? That Gentiles, who did not pursue righteousness, have attained to righteousness, even the righteousness of faith.

Becoming righteous has been and continues be one of the major differences between salvation through Yeshua and all other religions worldwide.

Judaism teaches that one becomes righteous through certain spiritual activities.

Yeshua made the startling claim that one cannot "become" righteous through a change of behavior. Instead, righteousness is the result, or the effect, of salvation by God's grace through faith in His atoning sacrifice. Christ's righteousness would be imparted to the Believer, thus enabling him to enter into the Kingdom of God.

Philippians 3:8-9

I consider everything a loss because of the surpassing worth of knowing Christ Jesus my Lord, for whose sake I have lost all things. I consider them garbage, that I may gain Christ and be found in him, not having a righteousness of my own that comes from the law, but that which is through faith in Christ—the righteousness that comes from God on the basis of faith.

PRAY FOR ALL JEWS TO RECOGNIZE THAT GOD WILL NOT ACCEPT THEIR ATTEMPTS TO BE RIGHTEOUS.

Day 22

When the Gentiles began believing in Yeshua, there was a great debate. Everyone asked the same questions:

- Did Gentiles have to become Jews?
- Did the Gentiles have to follow the laws of Moses and Jewish traditions?

But the larger questions were:

- Why did God allow Gentiles who followed pagan religions to be suddenly considered righteous in Yeshua?
- Why were Gentile and Jewish followers of Yeshua equal?

The problem is clear. While Israel was working hard "pursuing" a way to *become* righteous, the Gentiles willingly accepted the *gift* of God's righteousness.

Romans 9:31

Israel, pursuing the law of righteousness, has not attained to the law of righteousness.

PRAY FOR THE REMNANT OF ISRAEL WHO
WILL ACCEPT YESHUA AS MESSIAH.

Day 23

Paul answers the question, "Why didn't the Jewish people find God's offer of righteousness when they were so eagerly looking for it?"

Romans 9:32-33

Why? Because they did not seek it by faith, but as it were, by the works of the law. For they stumbled at that stumbling stone.

As it is written:

"Behold, I lay in Zion a stumbling stone and rock of offense, and whoever believes on Him will not be put to shame."

The stone that caused the Jewish people to stumble is Yeshua, the Messiah.

PRAY FOR THE JEWISH PEOPLE TO ACCEPT AND NOT STUMBLE OVER THE STONE THAT IS YESHUA.

Day 24

The prophet Isaiah was the first to refer to the Messiah as a stone that would cause the Jewish people to stumble and take offense.

Isaiah 8:14-15

"He will be as a sanctuary,
But a stone of stumbling and a rock of offense
To both the houses of Israel,
As a trap and a snare to the inhabitants of Jerusalem.
And many among them shall stumble;
They shall fall and be broken,
Be snared and taken."

PRAY ISRAEL WILL STOP STUMBLING
OVER THE STONE OF OFFENSE.

Day 25

The second time the prophet Isaiah described the coming Messiah as a stone, it was to contrast God's way of righteousness through faith with Israel's way through works and dependence on other nations.

Israel had been desperately trying to find help by making covenants with other nations. But God considered those covenants "Covenants of Death"—covenants that He would destroy, leaving Israel helpless and hopeless.

Isaiah 28:16-19

Therefore thus says the LORD God:

> *"Behold, I lay in Zion a stone for a foundation,*
> *A tried stone, a precious cornerstone, a sure foundation;*
> *Whoever believes will not act hastily.*
> *Your covenant with death will be annulled,*
> *And your agreement with Sheol will not stand;*
> *When the overflowing scourge passes through,*
> *Then you will be trampled down by it.*
> *As often as it goes out it will take you;*
> *For morning by morning it will pass over,*
> *And by day and by night;*
> *It will be a terror just to understand the report."*

True security can only come from faith in the God of Israel. Only the New Covenant in Yeshua can bring righteousness, redemption, and salvation.

PRAY FOR ISRAEL TO FIND HOPE, HELP, AND REST
IN THE PRECIOUS CORNERSTONE, YESHUA.

Day 26

Job had spent his life fearing God and trying to be righteous through good deeds and sacrifice. He was confused by the suddenness of his terrible sufferings. The only explanation his friends offered was that Job had sinned.

Job 18:5-21

"The light of the wicked indeed goes out,
And the flame of his fire does not shine.
The light is dark in his tent,
And his lamp beside him is put out.
The steps of his strength are shortened,
And his own counsel casts him down.
For he is cast into a net by his own feet,
And he walks into a snare.
The net takes him by the heel,
And a snare lays hold of him.
A noose is hidden for him on the ground,
And a trap for him in the road.
Terrors frighten him on every side,
And drive him to his feet.
His strength is starved,
And destruction is ready at his side.
It devours patches of his skin;
The firstborn of death devours his limbs.
He is uprooted from the shelter of his tent,
And they parade him before the king of terrors.
They dwell in his tent who are none of his;
Brimstone is scattered on his dwelling.

His roots are dried out below,
And his branch withers above.
The memory of him perishes from the earth,
And he has no name among the renowned.
He is driven from light into darkness,
And chased out of the world.
He has neither son nor posterity among his people,
Nor any remaining in his dwellings.
Those in the west are astonished at his day,
As those in the east are frightened.
Surely such are the dwellings of the wicked,
And this is the place of him who does not know God."

Of course, we know the reason for Job's troubles. He hadn't sinned. In fact, God had called him "blameless and upright" (Job 1:8). But God had a lesson for Job, his friends, Satan, and even for us.

The same is true for Israel. Although Israel's sufferings are often the result of her disobedience, sometimes they reveal God's faithfulness to her despite her disobedience.

PRAY FOR ISRAEL TO FIND RIGHTEOUSNESS BY
GOD'S GRACE THROUGH FAITH IN YESHUA.

Day 27

In the midst of contemplating the plight of his brethren who were trying in vain to be righteous before God, Paul seems to change gears.

Romans 10:1

Brethren, my heart's desire and prayer to God for Israel is that they may be saved.

Paul's passion for his brethren of the flesh led him to pray for them. His passion for Yeshua led him to proclaim Him to them. A heart of love can do nothing else.

PRAY FOR OPPORTUNITIES TO PRAY FOR ISRAEL'S SALVATION AND TO PROCLAIM THE GOSPEL TO HER.

Day 28

Paul grieved because the religious Jews had zeal, enthusiasm, and determination to follow God, but they didn't *know* Him.

Romans 10:2

For I bear them witness that they have zeal for God, but not according to knowledge.

We often miss the richness of the original languages of Scripture. Although we have many scholarly translations and dictionaries, we are often more influenced by our own cultural understanding of the words. The Greek concept of "knowledge" is worth examining.

The Greek word for knowledge used in this verse, ἐπίγνωσιν [*epegnoses*], might sound a bit familiar because you've heard one of its derivatives, [*gnosis*], from which we get the word "Gnosticism." But actually, the word comes from two primary words:

ἐπί [*epē'*] is a preposition that essentially means *laying something on top of something else*—for instance, when a picture is painted over a previous one. The context here relates to time and space.[9]

γινώσκω [*genosko*] is a verb meaning to "to get to know, perceive" through experience.[10] This word is similar to the Hebrew ידע [yada'] as it relates to an intimate knowledge coming from an intimate, personal relationship.

Paul grieves that the majority of the Jewish people lack a personal, intimate understanding of who Yeshua is. Because of their rebellion, they have been blinded by God, and because of their rejection of the Holy Spirit, they have been unable to perceive or recognize Him. This blindness fulfills a prophecy of Isaiah.

Isaiah 42:20

"You have seen many things, but you pay no attention; your ears are open, but you do not listen." (NIV)

PRAY FOR GOD TO LIFT ISRAEL'S
BLINDNESS SO THAT SHE CAN
KNOW HER SAVIOR.

Day 29

Paul's grievance is not that the Jews seek righteousness, but with the way they try to obtain it.

Romans 10:2-3

For I bear them (Israel) witness that they have zeal for God, but not according to knowledge. For they being ignorant of God's righteousness, and seeking to establish their own righteousness, have not submitted to the righteousness of God.

From eternity past, God Himself designed the only way mankind could be saved: through the atonement of Yeshua.

Isaiah 53:10-11

Yet it pleased the LORD to bruise Him;
He has put Him to grief.
When You make His soul an offering for sin,
He shall see His seed, He shall prolong His days,
And the pleasure of the LORD shall prosper in His hand.
He shall see the labor of His soul, and be satisfied.
By His knowledge My righteous Servant shall justify many,
For He shall bear their iniquities.

The atoning sacrifice of Yeshua, God the Son, satisfied God's loving mercy to save sinners without violating His own righteousness.

PRAY FOR THE SALVATION OF ISRAEL BY GOD'S
GRACE THROUGH FAITH IN YESHUA.

Day 30

So often, people don't know what they don't know. This was true in Paul's time, and it's true today.

Israel rejected the revelation of Yeshua and was thus ignorant of God's offered righteousness.

Romans 10:3

For they being ignorant of God's righteousness, and seeking to establish their own righteousness have not submitted to the righteousness of God.

Many Jews over the centuries have been sincere, but they are sincerely wrong. Sincere but wrong beliefs will bring disaster.

The same was true of Job's friends who had a false understanding of God's grace and mercy. God criticized the friends for judging Job based on their concept of righteousness instead of on God's character of grace and mercy.

Job 4:17-19

"Can a mortal be more righteous than God?
Can a man be more pure than his Maker?
If He puts no trust in His servants,
If He charges His angels with error,
How much more those who dwell in houses of clay,
Whose foundation is in the dust,
Who are crushed before a moth?"

The result of spiritual blindness caused by rebellion, religion, or even tradition is a downward spiral.

PRAY FOR ISRAEL TO HAVE A
REVELATION OF HER MESSIAH.

Day 31

We're still looking at Romans 10:3 and considering the word **righteous**.

Righteous in both Hebrew צָדֵיק [*tsadek*] and Greek δίκαιος [*dekios*] means *to be accepted, to be right, and to be approved by God.*[11]

God's standards are so high that man cannot achieve righteousness by his own efforts. But righteousness is the only basis by which man can be justified by God.

So Paul asks and answers the crucial question: "How can I be righteous?"

Romans 10:3

For they being ignorant of God's righteousness, and seeking to establish their own righteousness, have not submitted to the righteousness of God.

The Jewish prophet Habakkuk prophesied of a new method of attaining righteousness yet to come.

Habakkuk 2:2-4

Then the LORD answered me and said:

> *"Write the vision*
> *And make it plain on tablets,*
> *That he may run who reads it.*
> *For the vision is yet for an appointed time;*
> *But at the end it will speak, and it will not lie.*
> *Though it tarries, wait for it;*
> *Because it will surely come,*
> *It will not tarry.*

"Behold the proud,
His soul is not upright in him;
But the just shall live by his faith."

PRAY FOR ISRAEL TO ACCEPT GOD'S
PROVISION OF RIGHTEOUSNESS THROUGH
FAITH IN YESHUA THE MESSIAH.

Day 32

We're going to digress from Chapter 10 to look at Paul's earlier discussion of the righteousness that comes from God, a righteousness that could not be accomplished through the Law of Moses.

Romans 3:21-22

But now the righteousness of God apart from the law is revealed, being witnessed by the Law and the Prophets, even the righteousness of God, through faith in Jesus Christ, to all and on all who believe.

The impartation of God's righteousness through faith in Yeshua is the foundational principle of the Gospel and thus of Paul's teaching. God-fearing people may seek righteousness, but sadly, their refusal to accept Yeshua as their atonement means they never achieve what they are seeking.

What is the righteousness that's available to all who would believe? Earlier in his letter, Paul declared that there is only one source of this righteousness that brings life: Yeshua.

Romans 3:21-22a

But now apart from the law the righteousness of God has been made known, to which the Law and the Prophets testify. This righteousness is given through faith in Jesus Christ to all who believe.

God would impart (give) His righteousness equally to Jews and Gentiles, but only through faith in Yeshua.

PRAY ISRAEL WILL BECOME RIGHTEOUS
THROUGH FAITH IN THE MESSIAH.

Day 33

Paul's presentation of the Gospel includes two other important words, **justification** and **salvation**.

Romans 3:22b-24a

For there is no difference; for all have sinned and fall short of the glory of God, being justified freely by His grace.

Justification. "Righteous" and "justified" both come from the same Hebrew and Greek roots. This might seem to imply that these words have the same meaning, but this is not the case for Paul.[12]

Paul uses justification in a legal sense, as an acquittal of guilt. He uses righteousness in reference to a godly character.

Salvation. The Hebrew noun יְשׁוּעָה [*yeshua*] is also used for "saved" and "Savior," hence the Hebrew name for Jesus. The Hebrew root is thought to come from an Aramaic root which means *having room to breathe*, a most appropriate description of the freedom that comes from faith in Yeshua. The Greek form σωτηρία [*soteria*] comes from the root σώζω [*sozo*] and is translated as *save* and *heal*.

PRAY FOR ISRAEL'S JUSTIFICATION AND SALVATION
THROUGH FAITH IN YESHUA THE MESSIAH.

Day 34

The third word in Paul's argument is **redemption** or its verb form, **redeem**.

Romans 3:23-24

All have sinned and fall short of the glory of God, being justified freely by His grace through the redemption that is in Christ Jesus.

Redeem or Redemption in Hebrew, גָּאַל [*ga'al*][13] or פָּדָה [*padah*],[14] and in Greek, ἀπολύτρωσις [*apolytrōsis*],[15] means *the act of regaining or gaining possession of something in exchange for payment, or clearing a debt.*

Redemption is the result of justification by faith.

PRAY FOR ISRAEL'S REDEMPTION AND SALVATION
THROUGH FAITH IN YESHUA THE MESSIAH.

Day 35

Let's briefly revisit Chapter 10 in Paul's letter to the Romans.

Romans 10:4

For Christ is the end of the law for righteousness to everyone who believes.

In this context and consistent with Paul's theology, "end" could be better translated as: "goal, fulfillment, or even termination."

Justification is immediate through faith in Yeshua, but righteousness is a process.

1 Corinthians 6:10-12

[And such were some of you.] But you were washed, but you were sanctified, but you were justified in the name of the Lord Jesus and by the Spirit of our God.

PRAY FOR STRENGTH AND PERSEVERANCE FOR
THOSE WHO ARE BRINGING THE GOSPEL TO ISRAEL.

Day 36

Paul's earlier discussion explains why Yeshua's sacrifice put an "end" to the Law of Moses as a means for attaining righteousness.

Romans 3:25-26

[Christ Jesus] whom God set forth as a propitiation by His blood, through faith, to demonstrate His righteousness, because in His forbearance God had passed over the sins that were previously committed, to demonstrate at the present time His righteousness, that He might be just and the justifier of the one who has faith in Jesus.

Two concepts can help us understand what Paul is teaching.

1. The sacrifice of Yeshua provided atonement for sin. That process is called "expiation."
2. The result of Yeshua's sacrifice was the removal of God's wrath, which is called "propitiation."

The Greek word for propitiation ἱλαστήριον from the verb [*hilaskomai*] is used in the Septuagint for the cover of the Ark of the Covenant.

PRAY THAT THE JEWISH PEOPLE WILL BEGIN
TO ASK, "WHERE IS THE ATONEMENT?"

Day 37

Yeshua's sacrifice satisfied God's wrath against sin. In modern terms, it was an act of reconciliation that enabled God's holiness and justice to be maintained. His sacrifice paid the penalty for our sins

God's holiness is intolerant of sin. His justice defines those who sin as guilty and deserving of death.

Ezekiel 18:3-4

"As I live," says the LORD God, "you shall no longer use this proverb in Israel.

"Behold, all souls are Mine;
The soul of the father
As well as the soul of the son is Mine;
The soul who sins shall die."

However, God's love and mercy provided a substitutionary sacrifice as the way to escape the death penalty. Yeshua's death was the substitutionary sacrifice.

PRAY FOR THE JEWISH PEOPLE TO BE CONVICTED
OF SIN, BOTH PERSONALLY AND AS A NATION.

Day 38

Although the sacrifice of Yeshua took place nearly two thousand years ago, the results are still effective today for all who believe. His is the only sacrifice that achieves the desired result: remission of sins and reconciliation with God.

In our modern era, people question or even challenge the reason for sacrifice. The Torah explains it this way:

Leviticus 17:11

"For the life of the flesh is in the blood, and I have given it to you upon the altar to make atonement for your souls; for it is the blood that makes atonement for the soul."

From the time the first sin was committed by mankind, God demonstrated that a sacrifice was necessary to cover sin.

When Adam and Eve disobeyed God and ate of the forbidden fruit, God killed an animal to cover the nakedness caused by their sin.

PRAY ISRAEL WILL ACCEPT GOD'S RIGHTEOUSNESS
THROUGH FAITH IN THE MESSIAH.

Day 39

Paul has explained "why" and "how" God considers a person righteous. This verse explains the "when." God considers a person righteous at the moment of conversion because of faith in Yeshua.

Romans 10:4

For Yeshua is the end of the law for righteousness to everyone who believes.

In God's Kingdom, both justification and righteousness are gifts from God and necessary to enable Him to be reconciled to the believer.

PRAY FOR ALL ISRAEL TO STOP TRYING TO
BE RIGHTEOUS IN HER OWN STRENGTH
AND ACCEPT GOD'S FREE GIFT.

Day 40

The first man who was considered righteous, accepted, or approved by God was Noah.

Genesis 7:1

Then the LORD said to Noah, "Come into the ark, you and all your household, because I have seen that you are righteous before Me in this generation."

Abraham was the next:

Genesis 15:4-6

And behold, the word of the LORD came to him, saying, "This one shall not be your heir, but one who will come from your own body shall be your heir." Then He brought him outside and said, "Look now toward heaven, and count the stars if you are able to number them." And He said to him, "So shall your descendants be."

And he believed in the LORD, and He accounted it to him for righteousness.

It's useful to remember that both men lived before the Law of Moses was given to Israel, proving that their righteousness was not the result of good works.

PRAY FOR THE RELIGIOUS AND DEVOUT TO
RECOGNIZE THAT RIGHTEOUSNESS COMES
ONLY THROUGH GRACE BY FAITH.

Day 41

The Law of Moses was glorious, but according to the prophet Jeremiah, another better Law would succeed it.

Jeremiah 31:31-32

"Behold, the days are coming, says the LORD, when I will make a new covenant with the house of Israel and with the house of Judah— not according to the covenant that I made with their fathers in the day that I took them by the hand to lead them out of the land of Egypt, My covenant which they broke, though I was a husband to them, says the LORD."

Yeshua Himself prophesied that He was the "end," or rather the "goal" of the Law:

Matthew 5: 17-18

"Do not think that I came to destroy the Law or the Prophets. I did not come to destroy but to fulfill. For assuredly, I say to you, till heaven and earth pass away, one jot or one tittle will by no means pass from the law till all is fulfilled."

PRAY THE RELIGIOUS WILL STUDY
THE PROPHECY OF JEREMIAH.

Day 42

Even though God's righteousness is available to all people, today both Jews and Gentiles still try very hard to become righteous through good works, study, and prayer. They often find it hard to understand and accept that righteousness comes only by grace through faith.

Romans 10:5

For Moses writes about the righteousness which is of the law, "The man who does those things shall live by them."

Paul refers back to the Torah, reminding the Jews of the impossibility of keeping the Law perfectly.

Leviticus 18:4-5

You shall observe My judgments and keep My ordinances, to walk in them: I am the LORD your God. You shall therefore keep My statutes and My judgments, which if a man does, he shall live by them: I am the LORD.

The structure of the Law was always "if…, then…." The Law demanded absolute and complete obedience.

PRAY FOR THE RELIGIOUS LEADERS OF ISRAEL TO QUESTION THEIR ATTEMPTS TO BECOME RIGHTEOUS.

Day 43

Next, Paul contrasts the righteousness of the Law with the righteousness of faith.

Romans 10:6-8

But the righteousness of faith speaks in this way, "Do not say in your heart, 'Who will ascend into heaven?'" (that is, to bring Christ down from above) or, "'Who will descend into the abyss?'" (that is, to bring Christ up from the dead).

But what does it say? "The word is near you, in your mouth and in your heart" (that is, the word of faith which we preach).

Paul is careful to say that faith does not *create* God's righteousness, but it is the *means* by which it can be received.

Paul then returns to the Torah, using verses that had since become idioms for describing something impossible.

Deuteronomy 30:12-14

"It is not in heaven, that you should say, 'Who will ascend into heaven for us and bring it to us, that we may hear it and do it?' Nor is it beyond the sea, that you should say, 'Who will go over the sea for us and bring it to us, that we may hear it and do it?' But the word is very near you, in your mouth and in your heart, that you may do it."

PRAY FOR SECULAR (NON-RELIGIOUS) JEWS
TO BECOME MISERABLE WITHOUT GOD.

Day 44

Finally, Paul explains how righteousness can be received.

Romans 10:8

But what does it say? "The word is near you, in your mouth and in your heart (that is, the word of faith which we preach)."

Earlier, we said that faith might be very sincere, but it can also be sincerely wrong. God judges us on the *content* and *object* of our faith, not simply that we *have* faith.

Therefore, Paul is very concerned with the content of our faith.

PRAY FOR ISRAEL TO LONG FOR A PERSONAL
AND INTIMATE RELATIONSHIP WITH GOD.

Day 45

A highlight of Paul's teaching is generally considered "the confession of faith." In this sort of confession, we publically acknowledge and agree with God and the "word of faith" preached to us.

Romans 10:9a

...that if you confess with your mouth...

The confession that Paul is describing is a public declaration of an inward determination of faith, a faith that has a total impact on a person's mind, will, and emotions.

PRAY FOR ALL ISRAEL TO CONFESS
HER NEED FOR SALVATION!

Day 46

Words come easily, but without substance, words have no lasting value. Paul was very specific about what we confess with our mouth.

Romans 10:9a

...that if you confess with your mouth the Lord Jesus...

We must confess our belief in the deity of Yeshua.

People have many different opinions about who Yeshua was including these suggestions: a good man, a good teacher, a prophet, a fake, a magician, a crazy man, or even a liar. But there is only one confession that matters: "Jesus is Lord."

That confession signifies our belief that Yeshua is:

- Equal in substance and character to God the Father.
- Fully God (deity) and fully man.

Ultimately, confession is individual and personal.

PRAY FOR ALL ISRAEL TO CONFESS
AND BELIEVE YESHUA IS LORD!

Day 47

Paul links the heart and the mouth. Remember, Jesus said: "Out of the heart the mouth speaks" (Matthew 12:34).

Romans 10:9b

If you confess with your mouth the Lord Jesus and believe in your heart that God has raised Him from the dead...

Paul is speaking here in spiritual shorthand. Although he's only referring to the resurrection of Yeshua, he is also including:

- The deity of Yeshua,
- His atoning sacrifice,
- His burial.

Yeshua's resurrection proved and validated His deity and His power over sin and death.

Romans 1:2-4

...the gospel he promised beforehand through his prophets in the Holy Scriptures concerning His Son Jesus Christ our Lord, who was born of the seed of David according to the flesh, and declared to be the Son of God with power according to the Spirit of holiness, by the resurrection from the dead.

God's gift of righteousness can only be given to those who fully believe and confess the deity of Yeshua and His death, burial, and resurrection.

PRAY FOR THE JEWISH PEOPLE TO START
READING THE PROPHETIC WORD OF GOD
IN THE TANAKH (OLD TESTAMENT).

Day 48

The rest of the verse promises that belief and confession will result in salvation.

Romans 10:9c

If you confess with your mouth the Lord Jesus and believe in your heart that God has raised Him from the dead you will be saved.

Many people confuse redemption and salvation. Although they are part of the blessing of faith in Yeshua, they are different. Let's look again at the meanings of **salvation** and **redemption**.

Salvation in Hebrew יְשׁוּעָה [yeshua], from the root יָשַׁע [yasha] is the continuous process of deliverance from sin, sickness, and sorrow that comes through faith in the atoning sacrifice of Yeshua.

The root in Aramaic describes and defines the word as "having room to breathe." Imagine being in a tight, restricted place, a place of bondage, and a place of distress and then being rescued. That is the picture of the Hebrew word for "salvation."

Redemption in both Hebrew and Greek means "a release through a payment." Redemption was the result of Christ's atoning sacrifice that paid the ransom to accomplish redemption. It was a singular, yet effective act (see Day 34).

PRAY FOR THE REDEMPTION AND SALVATION
OF ISRAEL THROUGH YESHUA.

Day 49

Paul's explanation of the content of a confession of faith expands on the words written earlier by the Apostle John.

John 3:14-18

"Just as Moses lifted up the snake in the wilderness, so the Son of Man must be lifted up, that everyone who believes may have eternal life in him."

"For God so loved the world that he gave his one and only Son, that whoever believes in him shall not perish but have eternal life. For God did not send his Son into the world to condemn the world, but to save the world through him. Whoever believes in him is not condemned, but whoever does not believe stands condemned already because they have not believed in the name of God's one and only Son." (NIV)

John and Paul agree that saving faith is "believing in," not merely "believing that." Although this distinction is often ignored, the difference is huge. Furthermore, most people ignore the contextual reference of Yeshua's statement—the bronze serpent (Numbers 21).

David Pawson suggests a more accurate translation of the Greek. Note the tenses of the verbs (emphasis mine.)[16]

"Indeed in just the same way that God the Father acted in love on another occasion, this time He did so for the whole rebellious human race, by sacrificing his only natural Son so that all who *go on trusting and obeying* him might never be ruined beyond recovery, but go on *having* everlasting and abundant life."

Christians need to keep lifting up Jesus, keep looking to Him, and keep believing in Him!

PRAY FOR THE CHURCH TO KEEP LIFTING
UP JESUS TO THE JEWISH PEOPLE.

Day 50

To Paul, confession by the mouth and faith in the heart are *both* part of the salvation experience. One cannot be separated from the other.

Romans 10:9-11

If you confess with your mouth the Lord Jesus and believe in your heart that God has raised Him from the dead, you will be saved. For with the heart one believes unto righteousness, and with the mouth confession is made unto salvation. For the Scripture says, "Whoever believes on Him will not be put to shame."

PRAY ALL ISRAEL WILL BE SAVED.

Day 51

Paul continues a thought that he started earlier in this letter to the Romans—that faith in Jesus is the only way to salvation for both the Jews and the Gentiles.

Romans 10:12-13

For there is no distinction between Jew and Greek, for the same Lord over all is rich to all who call upon Him. For "whoever calls on the name of the Lord shall be saved."

Paul's teaching does not differ from the earlier teaching of the prophet Joel.

Joel 2:32

"And it shall come to pass
That whoever calls on the name of the LORD
Shall be saved.
For in Mount Zion and in Jerusalem there shall be deliverance,
As the LORD has said,
Among the remnant whom the LORD calls."

PRAY THE CHURCH WILL PRESENT THE GOSPEL
IN A WAY THAT THE JEWISH PEOPLE CAN
UNDERSTAND YESHUA IS FOR ISRAEL!

Day 52

Sadly, many Jews today consider Christianity to be a "Gentile religion" and reject Yeshua as not being for them.

As we continue through Paul's letter, we must keep in mind his passion and concern for Israel to hear, understand, and believe the Gospel of Yeshua.

Romans 10:14a

How then shall they call on Him in whom they have not believed?

This verse begins with that little but important Greek word we've seen before, οὖν [*oûn*], which can be translated *therefore, consequently, or these things being so.*

Paul's argument is that all people are saved, justified, and redeemed by God's grace through faith in Yeshua.

"But," Paul asks, "how can Israel call on (trust, petition, hope in) Yeshua if they've never known or even heard about Him?"

PRAY ISRAEL WILL HEAR AND RESPOND
TO THE GOSPEL MESSAGE.

Day 53

For thousands of years, Israel had faithfully preserved the Word of God, written by the finger of God and given to them at Mt. Sinai. Throughout those years, many were equally as faithful in trying to obey the Law.

But by the time of Yeshua, the Law of Moses had been expanded to include traditions called "the Oral Law."

Although the Law and the Prophets foretold the coming of the Messiah who would bring a new, different, and better covenant, many were blinded and in bondage to these man-made oral laws and traditions and didn't recognize Yeshua. Sadly, this still holds true today.

Israel can neither call upon nor believe in Yeshua, if they have not heard about Him.

Romans 10:14b

And how shall they believe in Him of whom they have not heard?

The word Paul uses for "hear" is similar to the Hebrew word שָׁמַע [shama], which means *hearing with understanding that results in action.*[17]

PRAY FOR THE CHURCH TO BE COMMITTED
TO JEWISH EVANGELISM.

Day 54

So why aren't more Christians sharing the Gospel with the Jewish people?

Perhaps the reason comes from a statement that has been falsely attributed to St. Francis of Assisi. *"Preach the Gospel at all times and only when necessary use words."*

Fortunately the good monk never said this; in fact, he was a robust preacher. Nevertheless, this statement has negatively impacted the preaching of the Gospel for centuries.

Even today, there are many who suggest that it is more important to "preach the Gospel with their lives rather than with their lips."

But this is *NOT* Biblical. Worse, it is contrary to the Bible.

Romans 10:14c

And how shall they hear without a preacher?

It goes without saying that our lives need to reflect our life-transforming faith, but faith doesn't come from *seeing* the message. It comes from *hearing* the message.

PRAY FOR MORE WORKERS IN THE
FIELD OF JEWISH EVANGELISM.

Day 55

Paul argues that Israel needs to hear the Gospel of Yeshua so that they might call upon and believe in Him.

Paul then brings up the next issue, the importance of the "proclaimer."

Romans 10:15

And how shall they preach unless they are sent?

Enrico Caruso was a gifted Italian opera singer. The word Paul uses for "preacher" sounds amazing similar: κηρύσσω [*karuso*]. This Greek word is also translated "herald" or "publish."

Fortunately, the power of the Gospel is not found in the messenger's fine voice, but in the message itself. The message and the messenger are both sent by God.

PRAY THAT EVERY CHRISTIAN WILL
PROCLAIM THE GOSPEL TO HIS OR HER
JEWISH FRIENDS AND ASSOCIATES.

Day 56

Too often, the focus of attention is the messenger rather than the message. Perhaps that is why the Bible calls attention to the feet of the proclaimer, probably the least attractive part of the body!

Romans 10:15b:

As it is written:

> *"How beautiful are the feet of those who preach the gospel of peace,*
> *Who bring glad tidings of good things!"*

The beauty is in the "gospel of peace," and each of us has the privilege and mandate to proclaim it!

Paul references two of Israel's prophets who proclaimed God's redemption and salvation that would come through the Messiah.

Isaiah 52:7

How beautiful upon the mountains
Are the feet of him who brings good news,
Who proclaims peace,
Who brings glad tidings of good things,
Who proclaims salvation,
Who says to Zion,
"Your God reigns!"

Nahum 1:15

Behold, on the mountains
The feet of him who brings good tidings,
Who proclaims peace!

O Judah, keep your appointed feasts,
Perform your vows.
For the wicked one shall no more pass through you;
He is utterly cut off.

PRAY GOD'S PROTECTION, STRENGTH,
PEACE, AND PERSEVERANCE FOR THOSE
PROCLAIMING THE MESSAGE TO ISRAEL.

Day 57

We can almost hear someone challenging Paul and saying that God wasn't being fair to Israel. Nothing could be further from the truth. God has never stopped sending His proclaimers—the prophets who continuously bring His message.

Romans 10:16

But they have not all obeyed the gospel. For Isaiah says, "Lord, who has believed our report?"

Isaiah 53:1

Who has believed our report?
And to whom has the arm of the LORD been revealed?

Israel always had the opportunity to choose, but many persisted in disobedience. The rejection of the Gospel message is rejection of God Himself.

PRAY GOD WILL TURN ISRAEL'S REJECTION
TO ACCEPTANCE OF YESHUA AS MESSIAH.

Day 58

From the beginning of these chapters, Paul has been arguing that salvation comes only one way to both Jews and Gentiles: by faith.

Romans 10:17

So then faith comes by hearing, and hearing by the word of God.

An unspoken question between this and the next verse is: "Did Israel hear the Gospel in a contextual way so that they understood?" In other words, is her refusal an issue of hearing or understanding?

Paul actually answered that question already.

When those who have been sent by God proclaim the Gospel message, it will bear fruit. Perhaps the problem is that the message is not from God, but is the opinion, interpretation, or tradition of the speaker.

PRAY THAT ISRAEL WILL HEAR THE
PURE AND POWERFUL GOSPEL.

Day 59

Paul again addresses the issue of God's fairness in judging Israel, responding to any suggestion that perhaps the Jewish people hadn't heard the Gospel message.

Romans 10:18

But I say, have they not heard? Yes indeed!

The emphatic power of Paul's answer is somewhat lost in the English translation. Now, Paul uses this phrase as a double negative: μὴ οὐκ [*mā' ük*].[18] Paul is saying *"**Absolutely** they heard!"*

PRAY FOR GOD TO REMOVE THE SPIRITUAL
BLINDNESS FROM ISRAEL.

Day 60

Paul answers these questions and challenges in the way we should always answer questions—with Scripture.

Romans 10:18

But I say, have they not heard? Yes indeed!
"Their sound has gone out to all the earth,
And their words to the ends of the world."

Of course, the only Scriptures he had were the Tanakh (the Old Testament).

Psalms 19:1-4

For the music director, a psalm of David.

> *The heavens declare the glory of God,*
> *And the sky shows His handiwork.*
> *Day to day they speak,*
> *Night to night they reveal knowledge.*
> *There is no speech, no words,*
> *Where their voice goes unheard.*
> *Their voice has gone out to all the earth*
> *And their words to the end of the world.* (TLV)

PRAY THE MINDS, EARS, AND HEARTS OF THE JEWISH
PEOPLE WILL HEAR AND RESPOND TO GOD'S LOVE.

Day 61

You can almost hear another voice from Paul's audience complaining that perhaps Israel didn't hear with understanding. But Paul quotes the words of Moses in response.

Romans 10:19

But I say, did Israel not know? First Moses says:

> *"I will provoke you to jealousy by those who are not a nation,*
> *I will move you to anger by a foolish nation."*

God's offer of salvation to the Gentiles (the foolish nation) had three motivations:

- His love for all people (John 3:16),
- His desire to fill the earth with the knowledge of His glory (Habakkuk 2:14),
- His desire to provoke the Jews to jealousy (Deuteronomy 32:21).

God knew that the Jewish people would be jealous and upset that He'd allowed the Gentiles to know, love, trust, and worship Him by faith!

Today, rather than being jealous, there is still an animosity, an underlying resentment, or even anger among Jewish people concerning how the promises of God's blessings have been extended to the Gentiles.

Worse, some Gentiles believe that the Church has replaced Israel. But Paul corrects this theological premise throughout these chapters.

PRAY THE CHURCH WILL PROVOKE ISRAEL
TO JEALOUSY THROUGH HER INTIMATE
RELATIONSHIP WITH ISRAEL'S GOD.

Day 62

In his letter, Paul considers the Gentiles "foolish" because of their pagan worship and practices. The Psalmist also called "foolish" anyone who denied the existence of God (Psalms 14:1).

Over the years, Israel was greatly influenced by these "foolish" people, and that angered God.

Deuteronomy 32:16-20

They provoked Him to jealousy with foreign gods;
With abominations they provoked Him to anger.
They sacrificed to demons, not to God,
To gods they did not know,
To new gods, new arrivals
That your fathers did not fear.
Of the Rock who begot you, you are unmindful,
And have forgotten the God who fathered you.
"And when the LORD saw it, He spurned them,
Because of the provocation of His sons and His daughters.
And He said: 'I will hide My face from them,
I will see what their end will be,
For they are a perverse generation,
Children in whom is no faith.'"

Through faith in Yeshua, God would use these once foolish Gentiles to provoke the Jews to jealousy.

Deuteronomy 32:21-22

"They have provoked Me to jealousy by what is not God;
They have moved Me to anger by their foolish idols.

But I will provoke them to jealousy by those who are not a nation;
I will move them to anger by a foolish nation."

PRAY THE CHURCH WILL PROVOKE
ISRAEL TO JEALOUSY BY KNOWING
THE GOD OF ISRAEL BETTER.

Day 63

Paul used the Torah to answer the question about the "foolish Gentiles;" now, he turns to the prophet Isaiah.

Romans 10:20

But Isaiah is very bold and says:

> *"I was found by those who did not seek Me;*
> *I was made manifest to those who did not ask for Me."*

Isaiah 65:1

"I was sought by those who did not ask for Me;
I was found by those who did not seek Me.
I said, 'Here I am, here I am,'
To a nation that was not called by My name."

PRAY THE CHURCH WILL REPENT FROM PROVOKING ISRAEL TO ANGER AND PROVOKE HER TO JEALOUSY.

Day 64

Perhaps the most beautiful of all Hebrew words is חֶסֶד [*hesed*]. The word describes God's faithful love of Israel based on His covenant with Abraham. The best definition for *hesed* is *God's faithful covenant-keeping love*. Paul reminds his readers of God's *hesed* towards Israel.

Romans 10:21

But to Israel he says:

"All day long I have stretched out My hands
To a disobedient and contrary people."

As he does so often in this letter, Paul turns to the prophets for the basis of his argument.

Isaiah 65:1-5

"I was sought by those who did not ask for Me;
I was found by those who did not seek Me.
I said, 'Here I am, here I am,'
To a nation that was not called by My name.
I have stretched out My hands all day long to a rebellious people,
Who walk in a way that is not good,
According to their own thoughts;
A people who provoke Me to anger continually to My face;
Who sacrifice in gardens,
And burn incense on altars of brick;
Who sit among the graves,
And spend the night in the tombs;
Who eat swine's flesh,
And the broth of abominable things is in their vessels;

Who say, 'Keep to yourself,
Do not come near me,
For I am holier than you!'
These are smoke in My nostrils,
A fire that burns all the day."

And yet to this day, both Jews and Gentiles reject Yeshua, choosing instead to seek God "according to their own thoughts." They believe "all roads lead to God," or "all gods are the same." Ultimately, they are rejecting God's *hesed*, His faithful covenant-keeping love.

PRAY FOR ISRAEL TO REJECT ALL FALSE
GODS AND TURN TO YHWH.

Day 65

As a Pharisee, Paul had probably memorized the entire Old Testament. He knew that God's passionate, covenant-keeping love, *hesed*, was not a contradiction to His unchanging justice and holiness.

Another one of God's great mysteries is the seeming contradiction between His sovereignty (predetermination) and our personal responsibility; we must hold both truths equally.

There comes a time when He must judge and discipline even His beloved Israel.

Isaiah 65:6-7

"Behold, it is written before Me:
I will not keep silence, but will repay—
Even repay into their bosom—
Your iniquities and the iniquities of your fathers together,"
Says the LORD:
"Who have burned incense on the mountains
And blasphemed Me on the hills;
Therefore I will measure their former work into their bosom."

PRAY ISRAEL WILL KNOW GOD'S FAITHFUL
LOVE BEFORE SHE FACES GOD'S JUDGMENT.

Day 66

After God warns of the coming discipline and judgment, He gives the promise of restoration for those who will follow and obey.

Isaiah 65:8-10

Thus says the LORD:

> *"As the new wine is found in the cluster,*
> *And one says, 'Do not destroy it,*
> *For a blessing is in it,'*
> *So will I do for My servants' sake,*
> *That I may not destroy them all.*
> *I will bring forth descendants from Jacob,*
> *And from Judah an heir of My mountains;*
> *My elect shall inherit it,*
> *And My servants shall dwell there.*
> *Sharon shall be a fold of flocks,*
> *And the Valley of Achor a place for herds to lie down,*
> *For My people who have sought Me."*

PRAY FOR YOUR JEWISH FRIENDS AND
LOVED ONES TO SEEK GOD.

Day 67

Now comes another question: "Once the Gentiles received the gift of salvation through faith, what about Israel?"

Romans 11:1a

I say then, has God cast away His people? ***Certainly not!***

The answer to this question is crucial and reflects an understanding of God's character. Too many churches today are answering this question wrongly.

Paul practically screams out the answer, **"NO! Certainly NOT!"** He uses the same Greek words that he used before, οὖν μὴ [*oun mā*].

Those who teach that God has cast away His people deny or ignore His promise through Zechariah for the end time harvest of souls.

Zechariah 8:20-23

"Thus says the LORD of hosts:

> *'Peoples shall yet come,*
> *Inhabitants of many cities;*
> *The inhabitants of one city shall go to another, saying,*
> *"Let us continue to go and pray before the LORD,*
> *And seek the LORD of hosts.*
> *I myself will go also."*
> *Yes, many peoples and strong nations*
> *Shall come to seek the LORD of hosts in Jerusalem,*
> *And to pray before the LORD.'*

"Thus says the LORD of hosts: 'In those days ten men from every language of the nations shall grasp the sleeve of a Jewish man, saying, "Let us go with you, for we have heard that God is with you.""

PRAY FOR YOUR CHURCH TO PARTICIPATE IN THE END TIME HARVEST BY SUPPORTING JEWISH OUTREACH.

Day 68

Paul reminds his readers that he is proof that God has not cast away His people. Paul's "pedigree" is evidence that Jews are still loved by God and are saved by faith in Yeshua.

Romans 11:1

God has not cast away His people whom He foreknew.
For I also am an Israelite, of the seed of Abraham, of the tribe of Benjamin.

Israel was chosen to be God's witness so the Gentiles would know Him. God is consistent; He would not reject the people He chose to reveal His faithfulness!

1 Samuel 12:22

For the LORD will not forsake His people, for His great name's sake, because it has pleased the LORD to make you His people.

Psalms 94:14

For the LORD will not cast off His people,
Nor will He forsake His inheritance.

PRAY FOR YOUR CHURCH TO REJOICE IN AND
PROCLAIM GOD'S FAITHFULNESS TO ISRAEL.

Day 69

Paul understands that God's choice of the nation of Israel never meant that the entire nation (every individual) would be saved. Therefore, when we pray for "all Israel," we are praying for multitudes of individual Jewish people to believe and confess.

Romans 11:1-3

God has not cast away His people whom He foreknew.
Or do you not know what the Scripture says of Elijah, how he pleads with God against Israel, saying,

> *"LORD, they have killed Your prophets and torn down Your altars, and I alone am left, and they seek my life"?*

God always worked through a remnant as seen in the reference to Elijah.

1 Kings 19:10

So he said, "I have been very zealous for the LORD God of hosts; for the children of Israel have forsaken Your covenant, torn down Your altars, and killed Your prophets with the sword. I alone am left; and they seek to take my life."

PRAISE GOD FOR HIS FAITHFULNESS
TO HIS WORD TO ISRAEL.

Day 70

When answering the question about God's faithfulness in the midst of Israel's rebellion, Paul slightly changes God's response to Elijah.

Romans 11:4

But what does the divine response say to him? "I have reserved for Myself seven thousand men who have not bowed the knee to Baal."

1 Kings 19:18

"Yet I have reserved seven thousand in Israel, all whose knees have not bowed to Baal, and every mouth that has not kissed him."

Paul inserts the phrase "for Myself," thus indicating the action was totally of God. God protected those whose hearts and lives were completely His.

PRAY FOR THOSE CHURCHES WHO HAVE TURNED
AGAINST ISRAEL TO REPENT AND BLESS HER.

Day 71

God has always protected His remnant. Even today, God is keeping His remnant despite the moral decay and rebellion throughout the land and the people of Israel.[19]

As Paul points out again and again, God's choice is based on His grace, not man's attempts to attain righteousness.

Romans 11:5-6

Even so then, at this present time there is a remnant according to the election of grace. And if by grace, then it is no longer of works; otherwise grace is no longer grace. But if it is of works, it is no longer grace; otherwise work is no longer work.

PRAY FOR ISRAEL TO RECEIVE
GOD'S GRACE IN YESHUA.

Day 72

Israel's spiritual blindness is not a new condition.

Paul knew Israel's history and understood the cause and effect of Israel's blindness. He considers as "the elect" those who, with a heart for God, sought Him through faith by grace. The others insisted on seeking righteousness through their own works and were "blinded."

Romans 11:7

What then? Israel has not obtained what it seeks; but the elect have obtained it, and the rest were blinded.

Paul has no conflict between God's election versus individual free will. Only those who seek to blame God will ask, "Did those who rejected God do so because they were hardened, or were they hardened because they rejected him?"

PRAY FOR THE ELECT OF GOD TO SEEK
HIM WITH ALL THEIR HEART.

Day 73

Paul refers to Isaiah, who spoke to Israel during a time of crisis.

Romans 11:8

Just as it is written:

> *"God has given them a spirit of stupor,*
> *Eyes that they should not see*
> *And ears that they should not hear,*
> *To this very day."*

Israel had witnessed God's consistent deliverance from the enemy, yet just as consistently refused to acknowledge His hand. As a result, God blinded their prophets and seers. God used Isaiah to plead, challenge, and exhort the people to open their eyes and hearts.

Isaiah 29:10

> *For the LORD has poured out on you*
> *The spirit of deep sleep,*
> *And has closed your eyes, namely, the prophets;*
> *And He has covered your heads, namely, the seers.*

Before Isaiah, Moses also pleaded with Israel to recognize God's hand as Shepherd, Father, Provider, and Protector.

Deuteronomy 29:4

> *"Yet the LORD has not given you a heart to perceive and eyes to see and ears to hear, to this very day."*

PRAY GOD WILL REMOVE THE SPIRITUAL
BLINDNESS FROM ISRAEL.

Day 74

Although not in historical sequence, Paul first references Isaiah's pleading with Israel, then that of Moses, and here, David's.

Romans 11:9-10

And David says:

> *"Let their table become a snare and a trap,*
> *A stumbling block and a recompense to them.*
> *Let their eyes be darkened, so that they do not see,*
> *And bow down their back always."*

Psalms 69:22-23

Let their table become a snare before them,
And their well-being a trap.
Let their eyes be darkened, so that they do not see;
And make their loins shake continually.

God's unfailing love continuously gives Israel opportunities to recognize and seek His grace through faith.

PRAY ALL ISRAEL WILL RECOGNIZE AND
RECEIVE GOD'S GRACE THROUGH YESHUA.

Day 75

When many in Israel rejected Yeshua, God increased their spiritual blindness. Would that be the end of Israel's unique relationship with God?

For the third time, Paul practically shouts, **"NO! *Certainly Not!!"***

Romans 11:11a

*I say then, have they stumbled that they should fall? **Certainly not!***

PRAY FOR YOUR CHURCH TO PRAY
FOR ISRAEL'S SALVATION.

Day 76

Before we move on to the next verse, it's important to remind ourselves of Paul's focus: "Israel in God's plan of redemption."

Paul sets forth three major themes:

- Salvation is by God's grace through faith,
- God's faithfulness to Israel, and
- The uniqueness of God's relationship with Israel.

Deuteronomy 7:6-8

"For you are a holy people to the LORD your God; the LORD your God has chosen you to be a people for Himself, a special treasure above all the peoples on the face of the earth. The LORD did not set His love on you nor choose you because you were more in number than any other people, for you were the least of all peoples; but because the LORD loves you, and because He would keep the oath which He swore to your fathers, the LORD has brought you out with a mighty hand, and redeemed you from the house of bondage, from the hand of Pharaoh king of Egypt."

PRAY FOR A GREATER UNDERSTANDING
OF THE RELATIONSHIP BETWEEN THE
JEWISH PEOPLE AND THE GENTILES.

Day 77

Both Jewish and Gentile followers of Christ are needed to fill the earth with the knowledge of His glory through worship, praise, and the proclamation of the Gospel. As Pastor Chad Holland of King of Kings Community Jerusalem has put it, "Jews and Gentiles are like two pistons in the engine of God's plan of redemption."

Romans 11:11

I say then, have they stumbled that they should fall? **Certainly not!** *But through their fall, to provoke them to jealousy, salvation has come to the Gentiles.*

Sadly, many Gentiles forget one of their main assignments in God's Kingdom is to provoke Jews to jealousy. Instead, over the years they have provoked the Jewish people to anger, wrath, and resentment.

PRAY FOR CHRISTIANS TO FULFILL THEIR
PURPOSE IN GOD'S PLAN FOR ISRAEL.

Day 78

According to God's plan for the redemption of the world, there are distinctive assignments for Jewish and Gentile followers of Christ.

First, God promised that the world would be blessed through Israel.

Genesis 12:3c

"And in you all the families of the earth shall be blessed."

God gave His Word to the world through the Jewish people. Through Israel He revealed Himself and the plan of redemption—by grace through faith in a sacrificial atonement.

What could have brought the Gentiles greater blessings and riches than redemption through the life, death, burial, and resurrection of Yeshua?

As always, Paul answers his own question.

Romans 11:12

Now if their fall is riches for the world, and their failure riches for the Gentiles, how much more their fullness!

God's promise of the greatest blessing and riches for both Gentiles and Jews will come when Israel finally receives her Messiah!

PRAY THAT BOTH UNBELIEVING JEWS
AND BELIEVERS RECOGNIZE THE RICHES
OF GOD'S PLAN OF REDEMPTION.

Day 79

God's assignment for the Gentiles is still vitally important. The Gentiles are to provoke Israel to jealousy. Consider this potential process:

- Provocation to jealousy,
- Stimulation to curiosity,
- Providing an opportunity to share the Gospel,
- Resulting in salvation!

God's assignment for Paul was to proclaim the Gospel to the Gentiles. Yet he realized that as the Gentile believers would provoke the Jews to jealousy and subsequently lead them to salvation, his ministry would be enlarged!

Romans 11:13-14

For I speak to you Gentiles; inasmuch as I am an apostle to the Gentiles, I magnify my ministry, if by any means I may provoke to jealousy those who are my flesh and save some of them.

Despite Paul's extreme passion and concern for the Jewish people, today he is blamed and criticized by them for starting a new religion![20]

PRAY FOR BOTH JEWS AND GENTILES TO
FULFILL THEIR PURPOSE AND DESTINY.

Day 80

We must remember that if God chose the Jews to reveal His faithfulness, He would not and could not ever reject or forsake her.

God continues to use the Jewish people as His witness. Consider Israel's current history in light of His faithfulness:

- The rebirth of Israel as a nation on 14 May 1948,
- The restoration of the land from malaria-infested swamps and deserts into a modern country,
- The number-one startup nation,
- Leading international exporter of fruits and flowers,
- The gathering and return of the Jewish people from around the world to the land of Israel,
- Increasing numbers of Jews accepting Yeshua as their Savior.

What God is doing in, by, through, and for the Jewish people in the physical realm reflects what He is doing in the spiritual realm. When a person is saved by grace through faith in Yeshua, God brings life to that which was dead.

Romans 11:15

For if their being cast away is the reconciling of the world, what will their acceptance be but life from the dead?

Only God can bring life from ashes!

PRAY CHRISTIANS WILL RECOGNIZE—NOT
REJECT OR DENY—THE MIRACLE OF ISRAEL:
THAT GOD BROUGHT LIFE FROM THE DEAD.

Day 81

Romans 11:16

For if the firstfruit is holy, the lump is also holy; and if the root is holy, so are the branches.

There is a great debate today about Paul's use of "the root" in this passage. An entire movement continues to gain momentum based on the interpretation that the root refers to Israel or the Jewish people.[21]

I disagree with that interpretation.

As Paul continues, it is clear that "the root" is God. God is the Holy Root of the olive tree. God is the root from which the olive tree is nourished. God is the root from which both Jews and Gentiles can receive covenant blessings.

Therefore, the firstfruit and all succeeding branches will be holy.

PRAY THAT ALL PEOPLE WILL SEEK NOURISHMENT
FROM THE HOLY ROOT WHO IS GOD, NOT ISRAEL.

Day 82

Paul's illustration of grafting branches is contrary to nature and agricultural practices.

The natural process is to take a shoot from an olive tree that bears good fruit, though is not healthy, and graft it into a wild olive tree whose fruit is poor, but which grows strongly. The result is a tree with vigorous growth that bears good olives.

But Paul suggests the reverse to impress upon the Gentiles their dependence upon the root.

Romans 11:17-18

And if some of the branches were broken off, and you, being a wild olive tree, were grafted in among them, and with them became a partaker of the root and fatness of the olive tree, do not boast against the branches. But if you do boast, remember that you do not support the root, but the root supports you.

This passage clarifies that the Holy Root is God. It is God that sustains and supports both Jews and Gentiles.

But there is much more in this passage. Paul is addressing the negative, incorrect attitude of the early Gentile believers, still prevalent today, which holds that the Gentiles have replaced the Jews as God's "Chosen People" and are superior in all ways. Of course, this is also contrary to God's unique relationship with Israel.

PRAY THAT THE GENTILE CHURCH WILL HUMBLE ITSELF BEFORE GOD AND REPENT FROM ALL FEELINGS OF SUPERIORITY OVER THE JEWS.

Day 83

In this next passage, Paul continues to confront and correct an attitude that is still held by many believers—that God is finished with the Jews and that the Gentiles have become "the chosen." This is called "Replacement Theology." The personal motivations and prejudices of those who want to believe a lie distort the truth of Paul's statement.

Romans 11:19-21

*You will say then, "Branches were broken off **that** I might be grafted in." Well said. Because of unbelief they were broken off, and you stand by faith. Do not be haughty, but fear. For if God did not spare the natural branches, He may not spare you either.*

The misunderstanding comes from the little word "that" in the first sentence.

The Jews were not broken off because God needed "to make room for the Gentiles," but because they did not accept the offer of salvation by faith.

Paul is actually warning the Gentiles not to be self-righteous or proud. John Calvin once said: "We should never think of the rejection of the Jews without being struck with dread and terror."

PRAY AGAINST THE LIE OF REPLACEMENT THEOLOGY.

Day 84

Paul exhorts the Gentiles to consider that God's treatment of Israel showed **both** His mercy and His discipline.

Romans 11:22

Therefore consider the goodness and severity of God: on those who fell, severity; but toward you, goodness, if you continue in His goodness. Otherwise you also will be cut off.

Often people focus on only one side of God's character: either His goodness and mercy, or His holiness and justice. But we cannot divide God that way. When He passed before Moses, God gave a complete self-description.[22]

Exodus 34:5-7

Now the LORD descended in the cloud and stood with him there, and proclaimed the name of the LORD. And the LORD passed before him and proclaimed, "The LORD, the LORD God, merciful and gracious, longsuffering, and abounding in goodness and truth, keeping mercy for thousands, forgiving iniquity and transgression and sin, by no means clearing the guilty, visiting the iniquity of the fathers upon the children and the children's children to the third and the fourth generation."

Paul's reminder is as important to us today as it was then. We all need to recognize God's character through His witness, Israel.

PRAY JEWS AND GENTILES WILL RECOGNIZE AND
RESPOND TO GOD'S GRACE *AND* HIS HOLINESS.

Day 85

The next verse affirms that the Holy Root is God, not Israel. After all, how can a Jew be cut off from being a Jew? Impossible. But Jews can be cut off from God's covenant blessings through rebellion and unbelief.

Romans 11:23

And they also, if they do not continue in unbelief, will be grafted in, for God is able to graft them in again.

The psalmist experienced separation from God's love and blessings because of the rebellion of his people. But he knew that God's reputation depended on His faithfulness to forgive. Even today, Israel experiences a level of God's covenant blessings. How much more will come when the natural branches are restored into the Holy Root!

Psalms 106:4-8

Remember me, O LORD, with the favor You have toward Your people.
Oh, visit me with Your salvation,
That I may see the benefit of Your chosen ones,
That I may rejoice in the gladness of Your nation,
That I may glory with Your inheritance.
We have sinned with our fathers,
We have committed iniquity,
We have done wickedly.
Our fathers in Egypt did not understand Your wonders;
They did not remember the multitude of Your mercies,
But rebelled by the sea—the Red Sea.

Nevertheless He saved them for His name's sake,
That He might make His mighty power known.

PRAY FOR THE DAY WHEN
ALL ISRAEL IS SAVED.

Day 86

There is such good news for those who have been "broken off." One day, Israel's unbelief will become belief!

Romans 11:24

For if you were cut out of the olive tree which is wild by nature, and were grafted contrary to nature into a cultivated olive tree, how much more will these, who are natural branches, be grafted into their own olive tree?

Once again, Paul goes against nature. First, the wild branch never gets grafted onto the good branch. Secondly, never does that which was cut off get "regrafted in."

PRAY FOR ISRAEL TO BE REGRAFTED
INTO THE HOLY ROOT.

Day 87

The natural mind cannot understand God's unique relationship with Israel. We often see only Israel's rebellion and God's discipline upon her. Over and over, Paul exhorts the Gentiles to see Israel with God's love. God gave the Jews a spiritual blindness only for a season and for a purpose. Because of His faithful, covenant-keeping love, He has an appointed time when He will remove the veil.

Romans 11:25

For I do not desire, brethren, that you should be ignorant of this mystery, lest you should be wise in your own opinion, that blindness in part has happened to Israel until the fullness of the Gentiles has come in.

When Paul next says "all Israel," he is not saying that every single Jewish person will accept Yeshua as Lord and Savior. Paul's statement agrees with the prophets in the Tanakh (Old Testament); there will be exceptions within the nation of Israel.

Romans 11:26-27

And so all Israel will be saved, as it is written:

> *"The Deliverer will come out of Zion,*
> *And He will turn away ungodliness from Jacob;*
> *For this is My covenant with them,*
> *When I take away their sins."*

PRAY FOR ISRAEL TO RECOGNIZE HER DELIVERER.

Day 88

The Gospel is profoundly simple, although often misunderstood. God is love, but His love does not contradict His holiness.

The Jewish people have never been enemies of God, but of the Gospel. God's love for them has never wavered from the time He made a covenant of love with Abraham, Isaac, and Jacob.

Romans 11:28-29

Concerning the gospel they are enemies for your sake, but concerning the election they are beloved for the sake of the fathers. For the gifts and the calling of God are irrevocable.

We must never confuse the way God works with the nation with how He works with individuals, because what God promises, He fulfills!

PRAISE GOD FOR HIS COVENANT-
KEEPING LOVE FOR ISRAEL.

Day 89

God's plan of redemption is based on a symbiotic relationship between Jews and Gentiles.

- Gentiles were once disobedient
  - Gentiles NOW received mercy
    - Because the Jews were disobedient

- Israel now is disobedient
  - Jews NOW received mercy
    - Through the Gentiles who will provoke them to jealousy[23]

Romans 11:30-32

For as you were once disobedient to God, yet have now obtained mercy through their disobedience, even so these also have now been disobedient, that through the mercy shown you they also may obtain mercy. For God has committed them all to disobedience, that He might have mercy on all.

The end result will be God's mercy and salvation extended to all people!

PRAISE GOD FOR HIS LOVE FOR ALL PEOPLE.

Day 90

We began our journey through Romans 9-11 by looking back at Paul's outburst of praise (Romans 8:28-39). Now we end our journey with another explosion of overwhelming praise.

Romans 11:33-36

Oh, the depth of the riches both of the wisdom and knowledge of God! How unsearchable are His judgments and His ways past finding out!

> *"For who has known the mind of the Lord?*
> *Or who has become His counselor?"*

> *"Or who has first given to Him*
> *And it shall be repaid to him?"*

For of Him and through Him and to Him are all things, to whom be glory forever. Amen.

Then, in view of God's faithfulness and mercy to first to Israel and then to the Gentiles, Paul sees the only possible response and responsibility is to:

- Offer your body as a living sacrifice,
- Do not be conformed to this world,
- Be transformed by the renewing of your mind.

Romans 12:1-2

I beseech you therefore, brethren, by the mercies of God, that you present your bodies a living sacrifice, holy, acceptable to God, which is your reasonable service. And do not be conformed to this world, but be transformed by the renewing of your mind, that you may prove what is that good and acceptable and perfect will of God.

From the time of Paul until today, Christians are always in opposition to the culture. But God's Word stands unchangeable especially when it comes to His unique relationship to Israel and the Church's obligation to her. Thus we cannot ignore Paul's warning not to be conformed to this world that is increasingly against Israel.

Only a mind transformed and renewed by the Word of God will be able to stand firm and proclaim the truth.

PRAY FOR GOD'S GRACE AND MERCY AS YOU OBEY GOD'S WORD BY PRAYING FOR THE PEACE OF JERUSALEM AND THE SALVATION OF THE JEWISH PEOPLE.

Thus we come to the end of our journey together. I pray for you, Beloved, that you will know God's blessings as you stand with Israel and the Jewish people, regardless of personal inconvenience or challenge. I hope you will continue to use this prayer guide and join us on www.lunchtimeprayer.com.

For the glory of God,

The Controversy of Zion

For it is the day of the Lord's vengeance, and the year of recompences for the controversy of Zion. (Isaiah 34:8 KJV)

We are all caught up in turmoil. On every level—personally, nationally, and internationally—most of us are surrounded by confusion and chaos on a daily basis. In the hectic modern environment, Israel is often not a priority concern. But on God's priority list, Israel remains on top. Why?

I can suggest several reasons:

- God has irrevocably bound His glory and His reputation to Israel.
- The salvation of rebellious Israel is a reflection of the Gospel, of "life from the dead" (Romans 11:15).

Consequently, concern for Israel is not an option for those who love the God of Israel and believe in Yeshua, the Messiah of Israel. It is not an "either/or" but a "both/and" issue.

What do you need to do to show your concern for Israel? Besides the suggestions I made in the Preface, the single most important priority is to pray for her salvation. Secondly, I would suggest you pray for your church and your nation; both will be judged by their attitude toward Israel. The unbiblical attitude toward Israel so prevalent in the world today—and throughout history— is an outworking of the "controversy of Zion."

In our limited time and space, we'll examine this issue from three perspectives: the Lord's, the Church's, and that of the Gentile nations.

But first, let's answer some questions.

What Is the Controversy of Zion?

The controversy regarding Zion (aka Israel) is the manifestation of historical Gentile strife against Israel and God's eternal jealousy for her. This strife and jealousy encompasses the people, the land, and the city of Jerusalem.

What Are the Roots of the Controversy?

The strife of the Gentiles and the jealousy of God are rooted in God's sovereign election of Israel, and subsequent unique relationship with Abraham, Isaac, Jacob, and later, David. This relationship is reflected in what God calls "the Everlasting Covenant."

> *"I will make you exceedingly fruitful; and I will make nations of you, and kings shall come from you. And I will establish My covenant between Me and you and your descendants after you in their generations, for an everlasting covenant, to be God to you and your descendants after you. Also I give to you and your descendants after you the land in which you are a stranger, all the land of Canaan, as an everlasting possession; and I will be their God."* (Genesis 17:6-8)

It's important to recognize that this "everlasting covenant" includes both the nation and the land of Israel. These two pillars of the covenant lie at the heart of the controversy.

What Is the Result of the Controversy?

Let's look at the verse again, in several translations:

> *For it is the day of the Lord's vengeance, and the year of recompences for the controversy of Zion.* (Isaiah 34:8 KJV)

> *For it is the day of the Lord's vengeance,*
> *The year of recompense for the cause of Zion.* (Isaiah 34:8 NKJV)

For the Lord has a day of vengeance,
  a year of retribution, to uphold Zion's cause. (Isaiah 34:8 NIV)

Clearly, the result and the culmination of the controversy will be God's judgment, the Day of the Lord. The natural tendency is to recoil from thinking about the pain and suffering God will allow on that "Day," because we don't comprehend the holiness of God. Failure to understand God's holiness keeps us from grasping the depth of His pain when we reject His Son. We rush to the empty tomb without pausing to reflect on the Crucifixion.

But we cannot ignore that God's wrath must finally bring judgment to His creation. "That day" will be a time like never before and, since it will end the world as we know it, there will never be another day like it.

Now we're ready to consider the controversy of Zion from three perspectives.

The Lord's Perspective

The prophet Micah warned Israel of the Lord's contention with Israel:

Hear now what the Lord says:

> *"Arise, plead your case before the mountains,*
> *And let the hills hear your voice.*
> *Hear, O you mountains, the Lord's complaint,*
> *And you strong foundations of the earth;*
> *For the Lord has a complaint against His people,*
> *And He will contend with Israel."* (Micah 6:1-2)

God never made a secret of His anger against Israel for her continual rebellion and, ultimately, her rejection of Yeshua. And yet, in the midst of His contention and dispute, He never stopped offering His love and a way of forgiveness, deliverance, and salvation.

But the day will come when He must have vengeance for the sake of His everlasting covenant (Leviticus 26:23-33).

God has always used Gentile nations as His tools to bring discipline to His people when lesser forms of chastening failed to achieve His goals. At the same time, God then had to chasten those same nations because of their excesses. As Charles Spurgeon put it:

> "Never has God used a nation to chastise his Israel without destroying that nation when the chastisement has come to a close; He hates those who hurt his His people even though He permits their hate to triumph for a while for His own purpose."[24]

The good news, of course, is that in the midst of His judgment, God's promise of salvation shines as a beacon of light. The day will arrive when Israel's chastening comes to an end, all violence ceases, and weeping turns to joy (Isaiah 35).

The Church's Perspective

There are two major issues at the root of the Church's controversy with Israel. One is simply an issue of definition. Who or what is Israel? As an entity, "the Church" cannot seem to decide whether its use of the term "Israel" refers to a person (Jacob), a nation, and/or a land. My thesis is that Israel is all three.

The more foundational issue, however, is theological. While the Church appropriates the literal veracity of the prophecies regarding the first coming of Christ, it spiritualizes the prophecies concerning His second coming. In doing so, the restoration of the land of Israel and the regathering and salvation of the people of Israel become allegorized into applying only to the Church.

Starting with the Edict of Milan (313 AD), the Church made a monumental shift from the well-grounded premillennialism of the ancient Church fathers to the amillennialism or postmillennialism that would dominate eschatological thinking from the fourth century AD to at least the mid-nineteenth century.[25]

The people we are so familiar with—Augustine, Clement, Justin Martyr, Origen, and Jerome—were all party to this theological error. Later, Luther and Calvin added their voices to the choir, saying God was finished with the Jewish people. Even in the "Reformed tradition" of today, we are still facing what is essentially "Replacement Theology."

Gary Burge is professor of New Testament studies at Wheaton College Graduate School, long a top destination for acquiring a Christian education. In his book *Whose Land? Whose Promise?* Burge states:

> "Christ is the reality behind all earthbound promises…. Land is rejected…, land is spiritualized as something else…. The promise is historicized in Jesus, a man who lives in the land…. Whatever the 'land' meant in the Old Testament, whatever the promise contained, this now belongs to Christians…. The land was a metaphor, a symbol of a greater place beyond the soil of Canaan."[26]

Englishman John Stott was an Anglican cleric, prominent leader of the worldwide Evangelical movement, and one of the principal authors of the Lausanne Covenant in 1994. *Time Magazine* listed him as one of the top 100 most influential people in 2005. In one of his sermons, Stott stated:

> "The Old Testament promises according to the apostles are fulfilled in Christ and the international community of Christ [and have nothing

to do with a return of Jews to the land]. The New Testament authors apply the promises of Abraham's seed to Jesus Christ. And they apply to Jesus Christ the promise of the land and all the land which is inherited, the land flowing with milk and honey, because it is in him [not land] that our hunger is satisfied and our thirst quenched. A return to Jewish nationalism [in the form of a political state] would seem incompatible with his New Testament perspective of the international community of Jesus."[27]

Sadly, the list of similar statements by modern theologians and Church leaders could go on and on.

Yet what is forgotten by today's Replacement Theologians is the simple fact that the restoration of the land of Israel and the regathering of the Jewish people, **by the hand of God**, was promised in the same Old Testament that contains the promise of the New Covenant!

> *For I will take you from among the nations, gather you out of all countries, and bring you into your own land. Then I will sprinkle clean water on you, and you shall be clean; I will cleanse you from all your filthiness and from all your idols. I will give you a new heart and put a new spirit within you; I will take the heart of stone out of your flesh and give you a heart of flesh. I will put My Spirit within you and cause you to walk in My statutes, and you will keep My judgments and do them. Then you shall dwell in the land that I gave to your fathers; you shall be My people, and I will be your God. (Ezekiel 36:24-28)*

By propagating the heresy that God is finished with Israel, these Christian leaders and those who follow them are aligning themselves against the very God they profess to serve.

The Perspective of the Gentile Nations

The hatred of the unbelieving Gentile nations is demonically inspired. Since the Garden of Eden, Satan has inspired, cultivated, and used this hatred among the unsuspecting. Biblical history is replete with Satan's attempts to annihilate Israel—not only as the vessel God used to provide salvation through His Son, but also as the chosen vehicle for revealing His glory and faithfulness.

This hatred has only intensified, as evidenced by today's surge of anti-Semitism worldwide, fanned rather than diffused by political correctness, which accepts Islam as a religion of peace. Today, nations and churches are joining the BDS (Boycott, Divestment and Sanctions) movement that is attempting to increase economic and political pressure on the State of Israel to comply with the movement's goals, first and foremost to end "Israel's occupation" of the land God promised to Abraham.

Hatred for Israel and the desire to control the land and the prize of Jerusalem will only increase until the time of Jacob's Trouble and the Day of the Lord.

In his book, *The Controversy of Zion and Jacob's Trouble*, Dalton Lifsey gives this analysis:

> "This present age will not end before all nations are raging in great agitation over the question of the land of Israel and the city of Jerusalem.

> "God intends that the entire world be confronted over the issue of His sovereign choice of Jacob. God has predestined the issue of the Jew to be the premier issue by which the nations of the earth are tested and judged at the end of the Age. It is an ultimate point of divine contention that provokes an ultimate act of divine intervention.

"The 'Controversy of Zion' won't only polarize the nations. It will also sift the professing Church of Jesus Christ worldwide forcing her to either affirm the 'everlasting covenant' and embrace the dangerous stigma associated with it or forsake it, thereby encouraging the final assault on the land."[28, 29]

Political or Spiritual?

God is NOT through with Israel. The everlasting covenant He made with Abraham and repeated throughout the Scriptures has been on clear display down through the ages, to this very day.

While the arguments presented in this essay might sound politically tinged, I assure you the issue is not political.

Rooted and grounded in God Himself, the controversy of Zion is spiritual. Consequently, there is no power on earth that can mend a spiritual condition by means of a political solution.

God will bring the controversy to a close through judgment and deliverance.

Endnotes

1. Israel's uniqueness flows from her relationship with God. Consider the following:

    No other people group has maintained its unique identity despite being separated and dispersed throughout the nations of the world for thousands of years. A supernatural connection and bond persists among Jews regardless of their country of origin. We are family simply because we are Jews. A good example is the decision made by families whose loved ones were killed in a recent terror attack. The deceased were French citizens and had lived in France all their lives, but were buried in Jerusalem.

    Israel is unique in other aspects, as well.

    *   Her rebirth as a nation after her people were separated and dispersed for over two thousand years.
    *   Her land's restoration from a wasteland into one of the largest exporters of fruits, vegetables, and flowers.
    *   The restoration of the ancient Hebrew language with only slight modifications.
    *   The only nation chosen by God to fulfill His plan of redemption for all mankind.
    *   The only nation to whom God promised a particular piece of land they would steward until the return of King Jesus the Messiah.
    *   The primary nation whose history is recounted in the Old and the New Testaments.

2. The question of "who is a Jew" is still being debated, and everyone has his or her own opinion. Many Jewish people today believe being a Jew means being a physical, genealogical descendant of Abraham, Isaac, and Jacob. That notion is immediately challenged by the thousands of years of intermarriage

between Jews and Gentiles. In the world of the Old Testament, Gentiles could become members of Israeli society upon acceptance of the God of Israel. They were not considered Jews, but proselytes. Tamar and Ruth are examples.

The State of Israel was founded in the shadow of the Holocaust, which greatly influenced the question of Jewish identity.

"At present (2014), the definition is based on Hitler's Nuremberg Laws: The Right of Return is granted to any individual with one Jewish grandparent, or any individual who is married to someone with one Jewish grandparent. As a result, thousands of people with no meaningful connection to the Jewish people theoretically have the right to immigrate. It is generally understood that the Law of Return was drafted by David Ben-Gurion 'in the shadow of the Holocaust' so that "whomever the Nazis called a Jew and sent to the death camps would be offered refuge in the newly established State of Israel." Well known cases in the Israeli Supreme Court debating the question of "who is a Jew?" include: Brother Daniel v. the State of Israel, 1962; Funk-Schlesinger v. the Ministry of the Interior, 1963; Falasha Wedding Case, 1968; the Shalit Case, 1969 (also known as the "Who Is a Jew?" case); the I. Ben Menashe Case, 1970; the Zigi Staderman Case, 1970; the Langer Case, 1972; and the Beresford Case, 1989." See: http://knesset.gov.il/constitution/ConstMJewishState.htm

Adding to the debate is the question of converts to Judaism. The standards continually change due to the fierce battle between the ultra-religious who insist only a conversion under an Orthodox rabbi is sufficient, versus the more liberal Reform and Conservative movements.

Adherence to cultural norms and traditions is another aspect of Jewish identity, although this also varies from very liberal to very fundamental.

In the diaspora Jewish identity was traced through the mother, unlike in the Bible, where ancestry is traced through the father.

3. God gives His memorial name to Moses (Exodus 3:14) as: אֶהְיֶה [ehyeh], which means"I AM." The English YHWH is usually pronounced today as *Yah-veh* or *Yah-ho-vah* or simply *yod, hey, vav, hey,* which are the Hebrew

letters. However, Hebrew speakers hear something very profound. With a bit of manipulating the letters, they hear the verb in the past הָיָה [*hayah*], the present הֹוֶה [*hoveh*], and the future יהיה [*ihiyeh*].

4. The Hebrew Bible is organized into three main sections: the Torah, meaning "instruction," also called the Pentateuch or the "Five Books of Moses;" the Nevi'im, or the Prophets; and the Ketuvim, or the Writings. Taken together, it is often referred to as the Tanakh, an acronym formed from the names of these three main sections.

5. The Writings include Psalms, Proverbs, Job, Song of Songs, Ruth, Lamentations, Ecclesiastes, Esther, Daniel, Ezra, I & II Chronicles.

6. See: Numbers 14:2; Isaiah 11:9; Habakkuk 2:14, John 1:14.

7. For just a few references on the remnant of Israel: Isaiah 10:20-22; 11:11,16; 37:31-32; Jeremiah 23:3; 31:7; Ezekiel 6:7-9; 14:21-23; Joel 2:31-32; Micah 2:12; 4:6-8; Zephaniah 3:7-9,13.

8. "Righteous." Merriam-Webster.com. Accessed August 31, 2016. http://www.merriam-webster.com/dictionary/righteous.

9. "G1909 - epi - Strong's Greek Lexicon (KJV)." Blue Letter Bible. Accessed August 31, 2016. https://www.blueletterbible.org///lang/lexicon/lexicon.cfm?strongs=G1909&t=KJV.

10. "G1097 - ginōskō - Strong's Greek Lexicon (KJV)." Blue Letter Bible. Accessed August 31, 2016. https://www.blueletterbible.org///lang/lexicon/lexicon.cfm?strongs=G1097&t=KJV.

11. "H6662 - tsaddiyq - Strong's Hebrew Lexicon (KJV)." Blue Letter Bible. Accessed August 31, 2016. https://www.blueletterbible.org///lang/lexicon/lexicon.cfm?Strongs=H6662&t=KJV; "G1342 - dikaios - Strong's Greek Lexicon (KJV)." Blue Letter Bible. Accessed August 31, 2016. https://www.blueletterbible.org///lang/lexicon/lexicon.cfm?Strongs=G1342&t=KJV.

12. In Greek, the word group for righteousness and justification comes from the root δίκη [*deka*] meaning punishment, but is rarely used in the New Testament. Righteousness in the Old Testament is not a matter of actions conforming to a given set of absolute legal standards, but of behavior in keeping with the two-way relationship between God and man. Thus, the

righteousness of God appears in his God-like dealings with his people, i.e. in redemption and salvation. His righteous acts are extolled from the earliest times onward.

In the pre-exilic period, little is said about individual righteousness, the main concern being that men should remain within the aforementioned national righteousness. Access to it is denied to anyone whose life falls short of God's standards.

The exile, however, marks a turning point in the history of ideas, and thereafter, the Old Testament has no hesitation in speaking of the devout individual's righteousness before God. Before the exile, the pledge of God's presence among the people was their free, independent possession of the land, with his righteousness covering both the people and the land they owned. Afterwards, however, God's pledge is his gift of the Law, which provides clear terms of reference for righteousness between man and man, as well as a framework within which a man may share, and go on sharing, in Yahweh's righteousness.

With the rise of rabbinic Judaism, righteousness became completely identified with conformity to the Law. Many of the laws, particularly the ceremonial ones, were no longer relevant, but according to the rabbis, they were intended to train men in obedience—in particular, to provide a way for men to acquire merit in the sight of God. The passion for obedience thus became transformed into a striving for merit, to ensure one's part in the kingdom of God. Works of charity and works of mercy were considered especially meritorious, the former comprising everything that could be done by material expenditure, such as feeding the hungry, clothing the naked, giving drink to the thirsty, etc., while the latter were those requiring a moral effort, such as mourning with mourners, comforting the broken-hearted, and visiting those who were sick or in prison.

Brown, Colin ed. 1977. *The New International Dictionary of New Testament Theology, Vol. 3.* Grand Rapids: Zondervan.

13. Brown, Francis, S. R. Driver, and Charles A. Briggs, eds. 1979. *A Hebrew and English Lexicon of the Old Testament.* Peabody: Hendrickson Publishers. #1350 - gaal.

14. Ibid., #6299 - padah.

15. "G629 - apolytrōsis - Strong's Greek Lexicon (KJV)." Blue Letter Bible. Accessed August 31, 2016. https://www.blueletterbible.org//lang/lexicon/lexicon.cfm?Strongs=G629&t=KJV.

16. Pawson, David. 2012. *Is John 3:16 the Gospel?* Exeter: Imprint Digital.

17. For a more in-depth study of the context and revelation of God's memorial name, I AM, see the book *Who Are You? Moses Asks God.* Go to: http://novea.org/store/

18. μὴ οὐκ comes from two Greek Words: μὴ and οὐκ. "G3378 - mē ouk - Strong's Greek Lexicon (KJV)." Blue Letter Bible. Accessed August 31, 2016. https://www.blueletterbible.org//lang/lexicon/lexicon.cfm?Strongs=G3378&t=KJV.

19. The evidence of God's remnant is the increasing number of Jewish people being saved around the world. Sabras (native born Israelis) are leaders in evangelism reporting continuously of people being saved. The exact number of congregations and home groups is unknown, but estimated to be over 350.

20. Eisen, Yosef. 2015. "Splinter Groups." Chabad. Accessed 31 August 2016. http://www.chabad.org/library/article_cdo/aid/2713694/jewish/Splinter-Groups.htm

21. "Jewish Roots," also called "Hebrew Roots." The movement is increasing in numbers and in criticism. Since I do not agree with or promote the movement, I am not including citations.

22. See the book *Who Are You? Moses Asks God.* It's an enjoyable and inspiring read for an in-depth understanding of God's character. Go to: http://novea.org/store/

23. Morris, Leon. 1988. *The Epistle to the Romans.* Grand Rapids: William B. Eerdmans Publishing Company.

24. Spurgeon, Charles. 1988. *The Treasury of David.* Peabody, Hendrickson Publishers.

25. Allen, Matthew. 2004. "Theology Adrift: The Early Church Fathers and Their Views of Eschatology." Bible. Accessed August 31, 2016.https://bible.org/article/theology-adrift-early-church-fathers-and-their-views-eschatology#P19_2994

26. Burge, Gary. 2004. *Whose Land? Whose Promise?* Cleveland: Pilgrim Press.

27. Stott, John. "The Place of Israel," an unpublished sermon preached at All Soul's, Langham Place, London, cited by Stephen Sizer in *Christian Zionism: Road-map to Armageddon?*

28. Lifsey, Dalton. 2011. *Controversy of Zion and Jacob's Trouble.* Tauranga, NZ: Maskilim Publishing.

29. Joel 3:2; Zechariah 2:8; 12:2-3, 9; Daniel 11:30-32.

Back cover: Derek Prince. "Our Response to the Restoration of Israel." Accessed August 31, 2016. Used with permission. http://www.derekprince.org/Groups/1000066154/DPM_USA/Media/Radio_30/DPLR_30_Show/Restoration/Restoration.aspx.

Keeping in Touch

Email:

Novea@novea.org

Newsletter:

Subscribe: http://eepurl.com/bQaAAH

Websites:

www.novea.org

- Simcha blog: (Celebrating the Feasts of the Lord)
- Joanie's Jewels

www.lunchtimeprayer.com

You Tube:

Lunchtime Prayer for Israel

- Subscribe: https://www.youtube.com/channel/ UCE1cs4SLVgY3zHGadXXcJFQ

Novea Ministries

- Subscribe: https://www.youtube.com/channel/ UCBme4ZyxsZN6G6AgWkG0czw

Books and Media by Joanie

Available through: www.novea.org/store

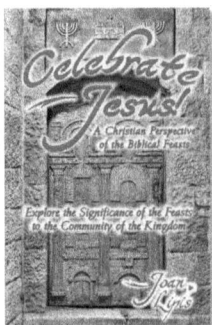

Celebrate Jesus!
Christian Perspective of the Feasts of the Lord

An easy to use resource giving the reader the biblical foundation and suggesting the personal application for each of the feasts. Good for pastors, educators and all who want to celebrate Jesus!

Celebrate Passover:
Three Tables Messianic Haggadah

The complete resource for your celebration of Passover. The liturgy takes you from the table of Moses in Egypt, to the table of Jesus in Jerusalem, and culminates at the banquet table of the Marriage Supper of the Lamb.

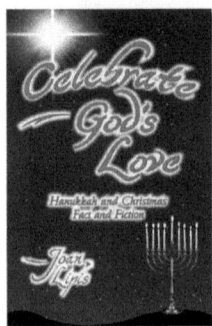

Celebrate God's Love:
Christmas/Hanukkah; Fact and Fiction

Confronts the myths and celebrates the truths of both holidays.

Celebrate the Lamb:
Messianic Perspective of Passover

Uses excerpts from *Celebrate Jesus!* yet corrects the English translations and expands the meanings of the Hebrew words for each holiday.

"Who Are You?" Moses asks God

Explores the words God uses to describe Himself through the original Hebrew and illustrations from Joanie's life.

Is God Through with Israel? Certainly Not!

A 90 day prayer guide based on Romans 9-11.

The Biblical Response to Israel (DVD)

www.ingramcontent.com/pod-product-compliance
Lightning Source LLC
Chambersburg PA
CBHW071128090426
42736CB00012B/2058